CHAPTER I.

The Discovery.

THE four little Ardens were playing whilst their papa and mamma sat at breakfast. It was winter, and so the breakfast-table was drawn near to the fire ; Mrs. Arden sat at one side of it, with little Tiny on her knee, and Mr. Arden opposite to her. He was opening and reading several letters which the postman had just brought. The other children were all in the window. Edmund and Johnny were very busy with some small carpenter's tools. Charlotte was making a polka for her doll, and Lizzie had got a book in her hand, but she did not seem to be reading very attentively. Charlotte was the oldest ; she was eleven years old ; Edmund was ten ; Johnny eight ; Lizzie seven ; and Mina, or Tiny, as the children called her, a very wee thing, just three.

The four eldest had been the day before to a tea-party with some other children, and they had a great deal to say about it to each other, but they tried to speak softly and not disturb their papa, whilst he read his letters.

" I should like to go to a party every night !" Lizzie said with a yawn, throwing down her book.

" So should I !" Johnny cried ; " all yesterday I was longing so for evening to come ;

AUNT ATTA:

A TALE

FOR

LITTLE NEPHEWS AND NIECES.

By the Author

OF

"TALES OF KIRKBECK", AND "LIVES OF CERTAIN FATHERS
THE CHURCH IN THE FOURTH CENTURY."

LONDON:
W. J. CLEAVER, 46, PICCADILLY.

MDCCCL.

Contents.

and now that it's gone I wish it hadn't come, but was still going to come."

"You can't have your cake and eat it,' Edmund remarked rather gravely, and gave a great chip to the piece of wood he was cutting.

"I know that, Mr. Wise," Lizzie said; "but some people *do* go to parties every night."

"Not children," Charlotte said; "only grown-up people; and I don't think that the nicest people do either. Papa and mamma don't go to parties anything like every night, and I'm sure there's nobody as nice as they are! But children never do."

"Carry Maxwell said she'd been to six parties this winter," Lizzie said, "and she's going to two more next week,—only think of that!"

"Well, I'm sure I'd rather stay at home, than go to parties with that tiresome, cross aunt of her's," Edmund said. "It was 'Carry, come here'; 'Carry, stop'; 'Don't eat that'; 'Don't make yourself hot'; or some bother or another all the evening. I never saw such a plague. What a rage I should be in!"

"How glad I am we've got no aunt!" Johnny exclaimed.

"So am I"—"So am I"—"So am I!" was echoed all round.

"Stho am me!" Tiny chimed in from her mamma's knee.

"What's all this?" Mr. Arden asked, looking up from his letters, and cutting a fresh slice of bread. "What are you all, even my great Tiny, so glad about?"

"That we haven't got an aunt, papa," Johnny, who was generally first to speak, answered.

"Not got an aunt!" Mr. Arden said: "why, pray what do you call aunt Mary, and aunt Emily, and aunt Henrietta?"

"Oh, but then they're not the sort of aunts we mean," Lizzie cried.

"How can I possibly guess what sort of aunts your wisdomships *do* mean then?" asked Mr. Arden.

"Why, papa, you know we've got no old maiden aunts," Edmund said; "that's what we mean. We haven't got a tiresome cross thing, like Carry Maxwell's aunt, to be always teasing and scolding us. Ugh! I'd rather have a little black boy!"

"Itty black boy!" Tiny cried, clapping

her hands, for she had a negro doll, which she liked particularly.

"How very flattering to maiden aunts in general!" Mr. Arden said. "But pray, Edmund, can you tell me why, according to your theory, all these unfortunate ladies are so unpleasant? I suppose there must be some cause for so remarkable a fact."

"Oh I can tell you, papa," Johnny burst out. "Tommy Broughton said it was because they were such nasty, cross, ugly old things, that nobody would marry them, and so there were maiden aunts to the end of the chapter!"

"I bow to the superior taste and information of Mr. Tommy Broughton," their papa said, making a low bow; "but do you know that I have got something to tell you, which,

after what I hear now, I am afraid will distress
you. I had fancied you would have liked it,
and was going to surprise you, but I'm afraid
you will all be sorry."

"What is it, papa?" "Oh what is it?"
"Do tell us quickly!"—and the children
crowded round their papa, and Tiny too cried,
"Do tell-a me!"

"Well, Johnny, you needn't pull my arm
quite off though, need you? at all events not
till I've finished my breakfast. Now will
you guess, or shall I tell you at once?"

"Oh please tell us, papa!" Charlotte said,
and the others began guessing a hundred
things, but they were all wrong; and soon
their papa said, "Why, it is a very sad dis-
closure to make, but I must tell you the
truth, that you have got a maiden aunt, and

not only that, but she is actually coming here, and will soon be with you."

Charlotte grew quite red with astonishment, and dropped her work; and the others jumped about, asking as many questions in two minutes as would have taken half an hour to answer.

"I don't mean to tell you anything about her now," Mr. Arden said, when the children stopped screaming at him. "You must wait patiently and see."

"Only please, papa, just tell us her name," Lizzie said very beseechingly, clinging round her papa's knees as he stood with his back to the fire.

"Shall we tell the inquisitive little beings her name, mamma?" Mr. Arden asked, smiling.

" Well, perhaps just that much you may," Mrs. Arden said.

" She is called aunt Esther," their papa said.

" Esther!   What a hideous name !" came from all four little voices at once.

" But, papa, why have we never seen this aunt or heard of her before?" Charlotte inquired.

" I cannot explain that to you, my dear," her papa replied; " you must be satisfied with knowing it now.   And so good bye; for if I don't make haste off to chambers I shall get no briefs, and have no beef and mutton for you or aunt Esther either !"   And giving mamma and Tiny a kiss, and blowing one to the others, Mr. Arden ran away in a great hurry.

The children were very anxious to get their mamma to tell them something about

this wonderful new aunt; but she said she
was not going to tell them anything, but
must order the dinner whilst James took away
the breakfast things, and she told the children
that Miss Marsh, their governess, would come
in ten minutes, and they had better get ready
for her.

Charlotte began to put by her work directly,
but Edmund and Johnny still kept jumping
over the footstool and crying out " Esther!
Esther! what a horrid name! To think of our
having a tiresome, ugly old maiden aunt
after all!"

And when they heard Miss Marsh's knock,
they ran to the school-room still shouting out
about their new aunt.

Charlotte was, as usual, tolerably attentive,
but the other three were rather more trouble-

some than usual. Johnny wrote " Esther is the best policy" twice over, instead of " Honesty"; and Edmund, when he was asked what was the name of King Charles the First's Queen, answered " Esther", which set all the others off laughing so, that Miss Marsh was obliged to look very grave, and say that she could not have any play till the lessons were done.

Miss Marsh only stayed till twelve o'clock, and then the children went out walking with Tiny and their nurse Moss (who had nursed them all as little babies), and Emma the nursery maid.

They had soon told Moss and Emma all about the ugly old aunt, Esther, who was coming to plague them, and Moss listened and laughed; but when they questioned her, she either could not, or would not, help them to any further knowledge. So they were obliged to be contented with their own guesses, and as they walked on by the Serpentine, they chattered away at a great rate.

They knew that their papa had a sister, but she had never been in London that they knew of, and they had hardly ever thought anything about her. But Edmund had looked in his papa's large bible, and there he had seen, besides the names of his papa and uncle Edmund, who was dead, "Esther Arden". So this was the new aunt that was coming to them.

" I wonder whether she really will be like Carry's aunt Sarah?" Charlotte said. " I should not like that, certainly."

" Like her! yes, and a great deal worse, I

daresay!" Johnny cried; "for Esther's a still uglier name than Sarah! I dare say she'll be a stiff puked-up thing, as old and ugly as can be, always finding fault, and scolding us, and never leaving us in peace for a moment."

"Will she be tall or short?" Lizzie asked.

"Oh, immensely gawky!" Edmund said, "and very thin, with a sharp red nose, and starched collars, I'm sure! I hate tall women! *Men* have a right to be tall," and Edmund drew himself up, "but no woman has any business to be a bit taller than mamma; she's quite tall enough, *I* think."

"Carry Maxwell's aunt Sarah, makes her wear backboards, and won't let her ride on a pony for fear it should make her crooked," Charlotte said mournfully.

"Backboards indeed!" Lizzie answered, with a toss of her head: "I should like to see myself in one! All the aunt Esthers and Sarahs and Deborahs in the kingdom sha'n't make *me* wear a backboard."

" And she'll always be down in the drawing room you know," Johnny said, " and I suppose her old head won't stand noise, and so we shall never be let play there. Mamma never minds a good racket at proper times, and I will make a noise, in spite of aunt Esther, that I'm determined!"

" I know I shall hate her, a nasty cross thing!" Edmund said, " and I'll do all I can to spite her, that I will!"

" Oh Edmund, don't say that," Charlotte exclaimed; " I don't think it's right, even if —if—I mean if aunt Esther is old and ugly,

I don't think we ought to hate her, because you know God made her as well as us, and our own dear pretty mamma, and besides—"

"Well," Edmund interrupted, "I like people to be pretty and good-tempered, and if they're not, why it isn't my fault that I don't like them."

The little Ardens went talking on about their new aunt, till Tiny grew tired of being left behind with Moss and Emma, and then they led her and played with her very nicely till it was time to go home.

When the evening came, and their papa was at home, and dinner was over, Lizzie and Johnny being gone to bed, the two other children stayed a little longer down stairs, and they could not help asking a great many questions about aunt Esther; but their papa was very tiresome indeed, Edmund said, and would tell them nothing at all, except that they must wait till Monday, and then they would see her for themselves. Monday —that seemed such a long while off, for this was only Thursday evening! But there was no help for it, and patience was their only friend; so Edmund and Charlotte went to bed, after trying to tell how many hours they had to wait before the day came when they would see aunt Esther.

Three whole days—that made seventy-two hours, and part of Monday—how much?

Their papa couldn't quite tell. Perhaps she might come about four or five o'clock. Then from seven, when they got up, till five, was ten hours; seventy-two and ten, that makes eighty-two hours. Only think of having to wait eighty-two hours !

"Well now go and sleep away eleven of them," their mamma said, "and then you will only have seventy-one to wait."

~ Charlotte and Edmund followed their brother and sister, and soon were fast asleep, and dreaming of all sorts of wonderful people who kept arriving all night, and saying that they were " aunt Esther."

———

CHAPTER II.

The Arrival.

THE little Ardens were accustomed to regular
hours and habits ; because their papa and
mamma considered that method and regularity
of occupation are very important in forming
a person's character, and enabling them to
be good and useful as they grow up ; and
although now their heads were very full of
the arrival of their aunt, still as all their
occupations went on just as usual, they had
no time for fretting, and growing discontented, as some children do when they are
excited by anything unusual.   Perhaps you

would like to know how the Ardens spent
their day in winter, at which time we have
made acquaintance with them. Their papa
was a lawyer, and obliged to be in London
during a great part of the year ; but they
had a nice, cheerful house in a square on the
south side of Hyde Park, which Tiny always
called *her* garden, and where they could go
by only just crossing the road, without getting into any crowded streets.

The children, began to get up at seven
o'clock : Charlotte and Edmund went every
morning, at eight o'clock, with their papa
and mamma to morning service, unless they
had been naughty the day before, and then
Mr. Arden said, he could not take them.
Johnny and Lizzie were very anxious to go
too ; and their mamma had promised that

whenever they got to behave quite nicely
and quietly at church on Sunday, they should
begin to go in the week, but at present they
must wait.   As their house was close to the
church they were never hindered by the rain,
even on dark winter mornings; and Charlotte
and Edmund were rather pleased to see it
raining ; so that Charlotte must creep under
the corner of her mamma's waterproof cloak,
and Edmund, in his pea-jacket, take shelter
beneath his papa's umbrella.   They thought
it very grand, and like grown-up people, to
go out in the rain.   Both the children were
very attentive and still in church ; for their
papa and mamma had taught them, ever since
they could understand anything, how great
reverence we owe to everything that is God's:
His House, His Ministers, His Book, and all

else that specially reminds us of Him. They left their Prayer-books in their seats, and were very careful never to let them fall, or get injured in any way.

When they came home from church they had their breakfast, and then all the children came downstairs whilst their papa and mamma breakfasted; Tiny generally sat on mamma's knee, and had little morsels of toast with orange marmalade, and sipped a little tea out of mamma's cup; but all the children were accustomed to see their parents, or other people, eating a variety of things, without ever expecting to have any, or thinking of asking for them.

At half-past nine Miss Marsh always came; she taught them writing, and arithmetic, and geography, and history, and grammar, and

French.   Three days a-week Mr. Walker
came to teach Edmund Latin; he had been
a very delicate boy, or he would have gone
to school before that time.   Johnny and
Lizzie were not all the while with Miss
Marsh; but their mamma heard them read,
and taught them some easy lessons, whilst
the others were with Miss Marsh, and even
Tiny would do her lessons too.   She could
say, very prettily, several little songs, about
the "Six little mice sat down to spin", and
"Once I saw a little bird".   Besides, Tiny
knew several of her letters, and could sit for
half-an-hour together pulling a needle through
a piece of canvas, and her brothers and
sisters thought her a most wonderfully clever
little woman for her age.   She was the
smallest of all small children; with a dear

bright little face, and great large blue eyes, and a quantity of very soft flaxen hair. When Edmund was learning English history he talked very learnedly about Tiny's being like the "fair-haired Saxons", so one of her many nicknames was the "little Saxon".

At twelve o'clock they all went out for a walk, if it was fine, and if not, they made a fine noise playing about the house. One favourite game was robbers. Edmund and Lizzie used to hide somewhere, and then spring out upon Charlotte and Johnny, who pretended to be a lady and gentleman travelling with their little girl ; and they used to have hard battles ; and Charlotte used to cry out, " Oh robbers, robbers, kill me, but spare my child !" Sometimes the child, or the mother, were taken prisoners to the robbers'

den ; and then they used to plot all sorts of
ways of escape; and Tiny was as full of fun,
and enjoyed the game as much as any of
them.

At half-past one they had their dinner.
All but Tiny dined downstairs at their
mamma's luncheon; and Miss Tiny dined in
state in the nursery, like a little queen, with
Moss and Emma to wait on her.

After dinner Mrs. Arden used to teach
Charlotte music; Lizzie very much wanted
to begin, but her mamma said she had not
time, and that Lizzie must wait a little
longer. If it was fine they all went out
again; sometimes one or two went with
Mr. Arden, and that they liked better than
walking in the Park; and there was always
so much to tell those who had not gone,

when they came home. If it was a wet day, and their mamma was not very busy, she sometimes played with them, or, what they liked best of all, she told them a story; but this was sufficiently rare to be a great delight.

Mrs. Arden generally went to evening service at five o'clock; but she did not take any of the children in winter; they had their tea at that time, and were all ready in the drawing-room by the time she came in; and then they were in such a hurry for her to take off her things, and get the lamp lighted, because, till dressing time, she always read aloud to them some nice book which they were not allowed to have at any other time. Charlotte and Lizzie always worked whilst their mamma read, and the boys either drew, or tried to make little models in card; sometimes Johnny did a little canvas-work, but he soon grew tired of it, and called it " girl's stuff".

Their papa never came home till just in time to dress for dinner ; and then the boys used to go into his dressing-room, and the little girls " helped" to dress their mamma. Sometimes Mr. and Mrs. Arden dined out ; and that the children did not like at all, though they were really very happy up in the nursery with nurse Moss, who was so kind and ready to do anything to amuse them ; but still they were never pleased to hear that their papa and mamma were going out.

I do not think five happier children could be found anywhere, though of course they had their troubles, which for the most part arose from their not being quite good in

some way. But no children are without
faults ; the great thing is that they should
have kind friends who are willing and able
to help them to amend, and that they themselves should be anxious to improve, and do
what is right.

In this way the days passed on till the
important Monday arrived which was to
bring aunt Esther. How the children talked
that morning ! and how eagerly they listened
to their mamma telling James that dinner
must be laid for three that day ; and they
followed her into the spare room which
looked towards the church, and saw how
nice she had made everything ;—the arm-
chair by the fire, and the sofa, and the little
writing-table, and book-stand, and a favourite
clock of Mrs. Arden's was on the chimney-

piece, and a scent-bottle of beautiful green
Bohemian glass, of just the colour which
Lizzie imagined that mermaids' hair was ;
and a number of other nice things, which
made the room look very pretty and com-
fortable.

" To think of all these nice things being
put for a cross old woman called Esther !"
Edmund said scornfully as he walked round.

By dinner-time the children had got into
a state of great excitement; Charlotte looked
sometimes red, sometimes pale, and was
very quiet, as she generally was when rather
nervous and shy; and the others were very
noisy. It was a raw, damp afternoon, and
rather foggy, so Mrs. Arden said the children
should not go out for a second walk. Charlotte fetched her work, and sat very close to

her mamma, as if for protection; Edmund got his paint box, and began a fancy portrait of aunt Esther; and Johnny and Lizzie stationed themselves, with Tiny, in the window, to watch for the arrival.

Many were the inquiries about the manner of aunt Esther's coming. Mrs. Arden told them that their papa was going to meet her at the railway station, and that she would most likely not come before five o'clock.

" Then I hope we shall be upstairs at tea", Charlotte said, timidly.

It was the end of November, and being a foggy day it grew dark, and Mrs. Arden had the drawing-room windows shut up soon after four ; and then the little ones grew very fidgety, as they could not look out for the carriage any longer. One after another

rolled by, and they were tired of saying,
" That *must* be it". At last a rumble came
very near—it stopped—yes, certainly it did
stop at No. 4. There was the visitor's bell,
so there could be no doubt ; and the door
was heard opening, and the steps being let
down. All the children grew silent. Charlotte crept quite behind her mamma's chair,
and Edmund put himself in an attitude of
defence near Tiny. In a minute the door
opened, their papa's voice said, " Come in
here, Esther"; and the much expected and
dreaded aunt Esther was in the room.

All the children opened their eyes very
wide; and Johnny fairly cried out, " Why,
mamma !" with downright astonishment.

Instead of the great, tall, stiff woman
they expected to see enter with an admoni-

tion on her lips, the lady who ran up to their mamma, and kissed her warmly and affectionately, was a very little person, less than their mamma even, and as far as they could see by lamplight, under a straw-bonnet trimmed with dark velvet, was a small, good-tempered face, with very white teeth, large bright eyes, and some glossy dark brown hair. A merry sweet voice said, "Dear, dear Mary, so here I am at last! And now for the children, I must have a good kiss from each!" and in another minute the little lady had given a good hearty buss to each of them, Tiny and all,—and then went back to kiss their mamma again.

Both Mr. and Mrs. Arden kissed the new comer, and looked very much pleased; and then Mr. Arden turned to the children, who were all standing lost in astonishment, and said, "Charlotte, aunt Esther thinks you want a back-board directly, or you will never be as tall as she is."

Aunt Esther began to laugh very merrily, and said, "Papa has been telling me some sad stories about you, and how much you dislike having an old maiden aunt, but I think we shall make it up between us by and bye."

"But you are not old at all!" Lizzie couldn't help saying.

"No, nor ugly either!" Johnny added very positively.

Then Mr. and Mrs. Arden, and aunt Esther laughed, and all the children began to laugh too, till Johnny rolled on the rug, and kicked with laughing, and Tiny clapped her wee hands, and shouted again with fun.

Then the children began to help aunt Esther to take off her things; one took her black velvet cloak, another her Chinchilla boa and muff, another her bonnet, and a fourth her carriage-bag; and they could hardly believe that the little, cheerful, good-tempered looking person, who appeared from under these wraps, could be the aunt Esther they had talked of so much. Tiny was soon settled on her knee, and was pleasantly engaged running her little white fingers up the nice soft curls which hung about aunt Esther's face. She seemed quite to approve of their new relation; and soon said in an oracular little voice, " Me shan't tall ou aunt Esta, me sall tall ou aunt Atta."

Everybody agreed that Tiny had made a great improvement on the new aunt's name, and she begged that all the children would call her aunt Atta instead of Esther; which name, she told them, she did not think at all pretty, any more than they did. " Indeed," she said, " I have not generally been called Esther, but a pet name, which I should think it very pert of my nephews and nieces to give me. Shall I tell you what it is ?"

The children all cried out " Oh yes !"

" Well then," their aunt said, " I have very often been called Pussy; only think of that !"

" Aunt Pussy !" Lizzie cried directly, and she could not help jumping into the back of her aunt's chair to stroke her hair, and see whether she would purr.

When Emma came down to say that tea
was ready, none of the children liked to go,
but they knew that they must; so they
quickly put by their things, and Tiny invited
"aunt Atta" to come up to the nursery, and
have tea with her. It was settled that aunt
Atta would be very glad to go to her own
room and rest, and so Tiny got her wish of
being carried upstairs in the new aunt's
arms; and as soon as she was deposited in
the nursery she informed Moss, "Of all me
aunts, me do like me aunt Atta de best," in
which the elder children were half disposed
to agree, although Charlotte explained that
it would be very ungrateful to like a stranger
better than aunt Henrietta, and aunt Mary,
and aunt Emily, who were so kind, and gave
them so many pretty things.

" Yes, but then you see they're so much bigger and older, and not the same thing," Lizzie added, not quite knowing how to enforce her argument.

" Well, as your new aunt is papa's only and very dear sister, I think you needn't be afraid of loving her too much," nurse Moss said, " and I dare say the other aunts won't be jealous. So now, Miss Lizzie, sit still, dear, and begin your tea."

The children began their tea, but they still went on talking very fast about aunt Atta, and how different she was from what they expected, and how certain they were that she was not at all cross. When they went down after tea, they half hoped that she would be in the drawing-room, but their mama said aunt Atta was resting; and she got the book, and began to read as usual. They were in the middle of *Tales of a Grandfather*, the French history, but this evening the children did not care as much as usual for it, and Johnny had quite forgotten how, the evening before, he had almost cried at having to wait to hear about Francis the First and his escape from imprisonment in Spain.

Mrs. Arden remarked this, but Johnny said, " I care for nothing now except aunt Atta; I want to see her again, and to hear more about her; I don't care a bit about the French history !"

Then Mrs. Arden tried to make Johnny understand how necessary it is not to give way to excitement which interferes with our regular duties, how it only unsettles and makes us uncomfortable, and does us harm.

" Why should your new pleasure of seeing your aunt, spoil your old pleasure of our reading?" his mama said. " You had better try to give your mind steadily to what we are doing, and then by and bye you will be quite ready to enjoy seeing your aunt. You and Lizzie shall come down to dessert with the others to-night on account of aunt Atta's arrival."

This pleased the children very much; and Johnny tried to give his attention to the reading, and not lose one pleasure because he had another in store.

That evening they all went to bed quite delighted with their new aunt. Tiny had sat upon her knee till dinner was announced, and made a scarf for herself with her aunt's long blue sash, and Lizzie had told her all about their lessons, and walks, and what they did, when they went to bed, and a great deal besides, and all the time Moss was putting her to bed she kept on chattering as fast as possible. "Do you know, Moss, *I* think aunt Atta quite pretty; not so pretty as mama though,—and I do like her long soft curls so much, and Edmund says he likes her because she wears white muslin. Oh when I'm grown up, I'll always wear white muslin! And aunt Atta can make purses, and do you know, Moss, she knitted her own polka, and she is going to knit some for Chatty and Tiny and me, and she says she will teach me to knit, and—and—a hundred things besides."

CHAPTER III.

Further Acquaintance.

THE next morning, when Charlotte was preparing for church, she began to wonder whether aunt Atta would go too.

" Perhaps she won't get up so early," she said to Edmund, who was waiting for his sister; " You know aunt Mary often says she wonders that mama can get ready so early as eight o'clock."

" If she's nice, she will get up," Edmund said, " I don't see why she shouldn't, as well as mama."

Charlotte had got her plaid shawl and her bonnet on by this time, so they ran to their mama's room, and there they found aunt Atta before them, with her bonnet and shawl on, all ready to go. Charlotte took her usual place by her mama, but Edmund walked by his aunt's side, and felt quite like her protector.

Once or twice, Charlotte could not help peeping up, to look at her aunt during the service, but when she saw how very grave and attentive she looked, Chatty's own eyes turned back to her prayer-book, and she tried only to think of the words of devotion which she was saying to God.

There was not time to see much of aunt Atta before Miss Marsh came, but the children were very fairly attentive to their lessons, and it was with great glee that Lizzie came running into the school-room, just as Miss Marsh was going, to say that mama said she thought it was going to rain, and that they might come and play in the drawing-room, instead of going out. So down they all came, and there, as they hoped, sat aunt Atta, but they were rather disappointed to see that her desk was open before her, and several letters at her side.

She looked up at them, however, and smiled, and asked Johnny to light her the taper, and then as she sealed her letters, aunt Atta said :—

"I have just done my lessons as well as you. I could not play before I had written my letters; but now we will have a good chat, and you shall tell me about a great many things. Only I must have my work; for I don't like sitting to do nothing."

In a few minutes they were all established most snugly, and then the children told aunt Atta how very disagreeable their idea of a maiden aunt was, and how their papa would not tell them anything about her, and so they expected an old cross aunt, but now they were so pleased to find her quite different.

Aunt Atta was very much amused, and laughed at their account. They wanted to know whether she was going to stay with them always, and Lizzie said she hoped aunt Atta would never go away again.

"*Never* is a long time," aunt Atta said; but at present she believed she should stay with them. Then she asked all about their different tastes and likings, and heard how Edmund was to go to school next year, if he had no bad colds this winter, and Charlotte

was to learn to ride perhaps, only she felt
rather frightened; and Lizzie wanted aunt
Atta to persuade mama to let her begin
music; and Johnny had so many things to
tell, that he was always interrupting the
others.

Aunt Atta seemed to be quite interested
in all their little affairs; she told Lizzie that
if mama had no objection she would teach
her music, which so enchanted the little girl,
that she set off instantly to run all over the
house to tell mama and Moss and Emma,
that she should begin music now, and aunt
Atta would teach her.

Charlotte told her aunt how glad they were
that she went with them to church in the
morning. " We thought perhaps you would
not like getting up so early," she said.

But aunt Atta told them that she always got up early, and that whenever she could, she liked to go to church.

"It seems to begin the day so well," she said, "and to make everything pleasant that comes afterwards pleasanter, and to take off much that is disagreeable in disagreeable things. I have been living some time lately with a very old relation of mine," aunt Atta went on, "whom I had to nurse and watch very carefully, so that I could not leave him much to go out; but there was a church near, where the service was at seven o'clock, and so I used to go there every morning, before my old uncle was awake."

"Oh how early!" the children cried.

"I hope I shall go to church soon," Lizzie said, who had come back now. "I mean

every day, for Johnny and I do go on
Sundays; but mama says we must learn to
be quite attentive first. I shall ask Mr.
Brantyre some day to tell mama to let me
go; she always does everything he tells her."

"Ah! but Mr. Brantyre won't tell mama
to let you go till she thinks fit," Edmund
said. "Aunt Atta, you must go and see Mr.
Brantyre, and love him as much as we do.
When I'm a man, I mean to be just exactly
such a clergyman as he is, and to do everything that he does. I don't believe there's
anybody else alive so good, except papa
and mama."

"And do you know, aunt Atta, he's my
Godfather," Lizzie broke in, "and he gave
me my beautiful Bible all bound in purple,
and my Prayer-book with a gold cross on it,

and sometimes he hears me say things, and teaches me, and I am so very very fond of him. I wish I could go and fetch him to shew to you."

"A pretty idea, indeed," Edmund said, "to go and fetch Mr. Brantyre to shew to anybody!"

Aunt Atta laughed too, and said she thought that would not quite do, but she should not much wonder if Mr. Brantyre came to see her, for he was a very dear friend of her's.

"Do you know Mr. Brantyre?" the children all asked in astonishment.

"Yes, indeed I do," aunt Atta said, "and love him quite as dearly as any of you can do. I have known him ever since I was a little girl of Lizzie's age; and one of the things that pleased me so much in coming to live with you was, that I should be near him again.   When I was a little girl Mr. Brantyre used often to stay with us; he was a great friend of your papa's, who is a good many years older than me; and he used to be very good to me, just as he is to you, and I used to stand at his knee and say the Catechism, and different little lessons to him."

" What a dear little thing you must have been !" Chatty exclaimed, and she threw her arms round her aunt, and kissed her.

Just then the door opened, and who should come in but Mr. Brantyre himself.   He was the Priest of the parish in which the Ardens lived, and the kindest and best friend they had.   The children all jumped up, and ran to meet him, but aunt Atta was quickest

of all; and the children seemed to like her
still better when they saw how much she
loved him, and heard him call her "my dear
child," just as he did them. Lizzie had
soon mounted his knee, and began eagerly
to tell him how they found that aunt Atta
had known him when she was a little girl,
and a great deal more, but he interrupted
her gently.

"Yes, Lizzie," he said, "and your aunt was
a good little girl, and always did what I told
her, and so do you generally; and now you
must all run away, because I have not much
time to spare, and I want to see her quietly."

Lizzie was rather disappointed; but she
jumped down again, and they all ran upstairs,
and began talking over aunt Atta as a little
girl, and Lizzie wondered whether she used

to be able to say "My duty to my neigh-
bour" without a mistake to Mr. Brantyre;
which Lizzie was very anxious to do, but
had not yet been able to accomplish, because
she was so apt to be very inattentive when
she was learning her lessons.

———

CHAPTER IV.

Johnny's Troubles.

AUNT ATTA was soon quite established in
Mr. and Mrs. Arden's house, and her nephews
and nieces rejoiced more and more in having
her. She was very kind indeed to them,
and was always ready to do anything that
was right to please them, but she did not
allow them to be troublesome, or ask over
and over again for what was once refused
them. They all knew that aunt Atta was
like their papa and mama in that; what she
said she meant, so that there was never any

teasing, or " Oh, pray do !" " Do let me !"
as is sometimes the case with children.

Aunt Atta had begun teaching Lizzie
music, and besides that she taught both the
little girls French, and several other things,
which gave Miss Marsh more time for the
boys. They liked very much for their aunt
to teach them, though she was quite as particular as their mama, and would have everything properly done, and not hurried or
lounged over. Sometimes aunt Atta walked
with the children, and that was great fun,
for she used to tell them all sorts of funny
stories. But what they liked almost best of
all, was, sometimes, when Mr. and Mrs.
Arden happened to dine out without their
sister ; and then aunt Atta dined at luncheon
with the children, and invited them all to

tea with her in the drawing-room, and played at some merry round game with them. They always looked for these evenings with great delight; and when they saw an invitation come to their mama they were always quite eager to know whether aunt Atta was invited too; and she used to laugh, and say how cruel it was of them to want to lose her pleasure for her; but the children declared, and their aunt did not say they were wrong, that they knew she liked a "good jolly evening with them best."

One day, at breakfast, aunt Atta had pleased all the children very much by telling them that, the day after tomorrow, papa and mama were going out without her, and on Charlotte's little table there lay a note in an envelope sealed, and directed to Miss C.

Arden.   It was opened, and found to contain
a regular invitation.

"Miss Arden requests the pleasure of Miss
Charlotte, Lizzie, and Tiny Arden, Masters
Edmund and Johnny Arden's company on
Thursday the tenth, at six o'clock.   A small
evening party."

Nothing would do but each child must send
a separate answer.   So aunt Atta found five
notes on her desk.   Charlotte's and Edmund's
were in due form.

"Miss Charlotte Arden has much pleasure
in accepting Miss Arden's obliging invitation
for Thursday the tenth."

Johnny's was "Master Johnny Arden is
very glad, and will like to drink tea with
aunt Atta."

And Lizzie's was "Dear aunt Atta, it will

be so nice. I shall come. Your own little Lizzie."

Lizzie held Tiny's hand whilst she wrote a very funny unreadable little letter which meant however that Tiny would come too.

Mr. Arden said he was quite offended that everybody seemed so glad to get rid of him and mama, and he thought aunt Atta was a witch, and he should prosecute her at the winter assizes for having unjustly bewitched his children. They did not in the least understand what he meant, but all the same thought it an excellent joke, and laughed very much indeed.

" Of course aunt Atta you only invite *good* children," Mrs. Arden said; and aunt Atta said, Certainly, she should tell her porter not to let any one else in. There was great talk and fun about this tea party all Tuesday and Wednesday, and the children were in high glee.

I have said that the little Ardens had some troubles, and those chiefly caused by their own faults, as most children's troubles, and indeed grown up people's too, generally are. Now Johnny sometimes had troubles caused by his being very pert and saucy. He was a clever little boy, and rather self-willed, and when he wanted to get his own way, he would do and say very silly things, so that Miss Marsh sometimes said what a pity it was that Johnny was not a dull child, and then he would perhaps be better. He was not often impertinent to his papa or mama, or to Mr. Walker, because he did not dare; but sometimes he was very saucy and spoke in a very improper way to Miss Marsh, or to Moss,

and Mrs. Arden had always remarked, that
when he was much excited, or had more than
usual pleasure of any kind, he was more apt
to become pert.   Besides this, Johnny was a
vain little boy, he liked to be thought well of,
and to be praised.   All children like praise ;
that is, they are anxious that their parents
and those they love should think well of them,
and be pleased with them, and it is right that
they should wish for that, and I do not call
that vanity ; but Johnny liked to be praised
by anybody whether he deserved it or not, and
he was often listening to hear what strangers
would say about him, and sometimes even
felt annoyed and unhappy if his brother and
sisters were more noticed or praised than
he was.   Charlotte was very different ; she
was a humble-minded little girl, and never

ready to think she did anything well, or that people could like her as much as the others; she thought Edmund and Johnny very clever, and Lizzie and Tiny very pretty, and thought every one must prefer them to her. Charlotte liked her papa and mama, or Mr. Brantyre or Miss Marsh, to praise her, and say she had done anything well; but if other people praised her, she generally grew very red and uncomfortable, and instead of seeking for praise, she would sometimes be quite anxious to shew that she did not deserve it.

Charlotte liked aunt Atta to praise her, for she knew she always meant what she said; and Johnny too liked his aunt to praise him, which she but seldom did, thinking that it was no kindness to encourage her little nephew's vanity.

Mrs. Arden had noticed that Johnny had been more saucy lately; Moss had twice complained of him, and Miss Marsh had more than once had to stay after the regular lesson hour was over, to try and bring him into order without making a regular complaint.

This Thursday morning Johnny began bragging, in a silly conceited way, how well he wrote; better than Tommy Broughton, a great deal, he knew; and he had heard aunt Mary say, yesterday, that cousin Georgy didn't write half as well as he did. Edmund answered him rather quickly, and then Johnny gave his brother a sharp answer.

"Now, Johnny, do not be silly," Miss Marsh said; "but, instead of talking about your good writing, let me see how well you

can do this sum.   Now then, set to work
briskly."

"I hate sums, and I know I write better
than cousin Georgy," Johnny answered with
a pouting face, and a pettish shake of the
shoulder.

"Then I'm sure you don't !" Edmund said.

"I tell you I do ; and I write better than
you, or than—"

"Hush, hush !" Miss Marsh said, "do not
say any more about it ;" and Edmund was
silent directly, but Johnny was excited with
indignation at his writing being undervalued,
as he thought, and he pushed his slate away
from him, going on as fast as ever he could
speak, "I *do* write the best a great deal, I
know I do, and it's only because you're such
a cross, unkind thing that you say I don't,

and I won't do my sums, and I hate you, and"—a great deal more which I will not repeat, for it was very silly, and worse—very wrong.

It happened that Mrs. Arden and aunt Atta were just going past the school-room door, and hearing Johnny's voice raised so high, they looked in; Johnny was still more vexed to be seen; but instead of calming him, his vexation made him worse, and he answered very improperly when Mrs. Arden spoke to him. She was obliged to take him away, and after keeping him with her until he was quieter, to leave him in the nursery, where, she told Moss, he must have his dinner, instead of coming downstairs as usual.

Johnny did not choose to seem sorry for a long time, it wounded his vanity; and so the silly little boy sat by the nursery fender, half sobbing, and refusing to play with Tiny, or answer Moss or Emma when they spoke to him, because he fancied it was more dignified to be cross !

Nobody took any trouble about him when they saw how it was ; and there he sat, very uncomfortable and unhappy. The other children could not make him speak to them when they came upstairs ; and it was not till dusk, when Mrs. Arden went upstairs to get ready for evening service, that Johnny seemed at all disposed to be good. Then when she talked kindly to him, and told him how very naughty such proud, sulky tempers were, Johnny's little heart began to soften, and he cried bitterly as he sat by her side and hid his face in the window curtain.

His mama went away to Church, for the
last bell was ringing, but she told Johnny to
ask GOD to forgive him for his naughty spirit,
and promised that she too would ask for him.
Mrs. Arden did not say anything about aunt
Atta, and the tea-party, but Johnny was
quite certain that he was not to go, he remembered what had been said about only
good children being at it, and though all the
day Johnny had been believing himself very
good, and sadly ill-used, he had now " come
to his senses," as Moss called it, and knew
that he could not be called a good boy.

He heard Mrs. and Miss Arden come
home; they just looked into the school-room,
and then he heard aunt Atta's door shut, and
in a minute his mama came into her room,
where Johnny still was, sitting near the

window with no light but from the fire, not
because he was sulky now, but because he
liked to be alone. Mrs. Arden saw by his
face that he was not naughty any longer, and
she kissed Johnny and spoke kindly to him,
and then she told him that he might go and
fetch Tiny to her whilst she dressed for
dinner. Before he went however, Johnny
slipped his hand into her's, and she saw he
wanted to say something, so she waited a
minute.

Then Johnny whispered very softly, " I
mustn't go to tea with aunt Atta, must I ?"

" No, dear boy," his mama said, " not
to-day. You would not enjoy it, if I said
you might ; for you would feel that you did
not deserve it. I am very sorry, for I know
it will be a great disappointment. But you

may go to aunt Atta's room before she goes down, and shew her that *now* her little Johnny is a good boy."

Then Mrs. Arden kissed Johnny again, and he ran and took Tiny very kindly and carefully to her mama's room. Then he went to the landing place outside his aunt's room, and stood there, unable to make up his mind to go in.

At last he thought that this was some of the silly pride, about which his mama had talked to him, so he made up his mind, and gave a gentle knock.

" Come in," aunt Atta said; and Johnny went in very slowly, and looking down. But his aunt met him and took his two hands, and spoke so kindly to him, that the tears came back into his eyes. She talked to him a little about his silly conceit and pride, and then she said,—

"I am so sorry that our tea party will be spoiled to-night, for we cannot be happy unless we are all together, I am sure, and Edmund in particular thinks he is to blame, for answering you hastily this morning. But now, before I go down to them, Johnny, we will sit down for a few minutes by the fire, and I will tell you something that happened to me when I was a little girl, which I think you will like to hear."

Johnny was pleased at the thoughts of a story; and his aunt sitting down in the great arm-chair, he squeezed in at her side, and looked up eagerly for the story.

"When I was a little girl, I was like you, very fond of being praised, and thought

clever," aunt Atta began:—" and I had a
kind but unwise old nurse, who used to encourage me in these naughty fancies. You
know, Johnny, that your papa and I had no
dear mama, as you have, to help to teach us
and make us good; and I am sorry to say,
aunt Atta was a terribly spoiled little girl!"

Johnny smiled, and stroked his aunt's
face.

" Your dear grandpapa let me do far too
much what I liked, and sometimes I gave
myself great airs, and was a very foolish
child. That was about the time that Mr.
Brantyre used to come and stay with us,
and I never liked him to see me in my
' tantrums,' as nurse used to call them.

" Well, it happened one day that I did not
choose to do any of my lessons properly, and

when my governess said I must stay up stairs,
instead of going down to dinner, I am
ashamed to say, Johnny, that I answered,
'I will not be treated like a baby,' and down
I went, in spite of her, knowing that my
good-natured papa would only laugh, and
say I was the veriest spoilt darling in the
world. So down I ran to him, and poured
out my complaints, and just as I had expected, he gave it all in to me, and I was
going away quite triumphant, when in the
window, where I had not happened to see
him before, sat Mr. Brantyre, looking very
serious and stern indeed, I thought."

"Oh, aunt Atta, how frightened you must
have been! I should not like him to look so
at me!"

"I was frightened, Johnny, all the more

because I knew very well that I was doing wrong; but Mr. Brantyre said nothing to me then, and I went back and told my governess that papa said I might come down to dinner. Our dinner was the grown-up people's luncheon time, and when Mr. Brantyre came in, I felt my face grow hot, and I could not look up at him. When my dinner was over, and I was going away with my governess, he turned to her, and asked if she would allow me to go out with him that afternoon. Generally, I should have been delighted to go, but to-day I did not like it at all, and went very slowly to get ready. He took my hand, and walked some way without speaking, till we came to a grassy bank under some old trees, and then Mr. Brantyre sat down, and began to talk to me about my naughty ways, and told me how GOD was always watching me, and how displeased He was at such ill-tempers, and then he told me to tell my governess how sorry I was, and to pray that I might be able to fight against the inclination to be self-willed, and I went home quite a different little girl."

" And were you never naughty again, aunt Atta?"

" Oh yes, indeed I was, Johnny, but the recollection of all my kind friend said to me always come to check me, and helped me to conquer my self-will. And now that I have told you my story I must go down to the others."

"May I tell it to them, aunt Atta?" Johnny asked.

" Yes you may if you like, though I don't

think it does the old maiden aunt much credit," aunt Atta said, smiling.

"I like it very much though," Johnny said, "only I can't fancy your ever being so naughty."

Thus Johnny went back to the nursery, and his aunt went down stairs; but the tea party was not nearly so pleasant as the children had expected, for they were all very fond of one another, and they did not like Johnny to be in disgrace. They asked aunt Atta not to tell them any pretty stories, as he was not there, and they did not beg to sit up an extra half-hour, as they usually did on these grand nights. When they went up stairs, Charlotte crept softly to Johnny's bedside, and when she found that he was awake, she kissed him very lovingly and whispered, " We begged aunt Atta not to tell us stories to-night, Johnny, as you wern't with us, so you havn't lost any."

" Dear kind Chatty!" Johnny said; and then Moss called to Miss Charlotte to come to bed, and she ran off, and very soon all the little set were fast asleep, forgetting all their cares and troubles.

CHAPTER V.

The Doves.

Spring was coming on fast, and the children enjoyed their walks in the Park very much indeed. Their aunt was often tempted by the bright sunshine to go with them, and then she used to tell them about all sorts of foreign animals and birds which she had seen; for aunt Atta had been abroad a great deal. They were all very fond of going to the Zoological gardens, and one fine morning as they walked round the Serpentine, they began to say what animals they should choose

as pets, if they might go and take what they
liked. Edmund said he should like a fine
black horse better than anything, and Johnny wished for a lion,—the fiercer the better,
it should only be quite tame and gentle to
him. Lizzie said she would choose a monkey,
and aunt Atta said she was a little monkey
herself. Charlotte thought she should like
nothing so well as a nice white dove, with its
plaintive coo-coo. Then they all wanted to
know what aunt Atta would choose. She
said that she had been very fond of a pet horse
once, and that she had also kept doves, but
of all animals there was none she liked
so well as a dog; and then she told them
about a favourite dog of her's called Duke,
which she had kept from a puppy till it died
of old age, and the very last thing it did

when it was dying was to lick her hands to
shew its affection.

Charlotte almost cried about poor Duke,
and they all agreed that if ever they had a
dog it should be called Duke too.

Soon after they were gone home, aunt
Atta came to the schoolroom and said, " Come
with me to my room, I have something to
shew you, but come very quietly and gently."

They all ran after her, and when they
were all in, she shut the door very carefully.

The children could not think what their
aunt had got to shew them, till at last, in
one corner of the room, perched on the back
of a chair, they saw a pretty soft-looking
dove, with a purple ring about its neck, and
a deep red circle round its large bright but
soft eyes.

An exclamation of delight burst from the children, " Whose is it? Where did it come from? What a dear pretty thing! Oh aunt Atta how did it come here?"

" Hush! do not frighten it," their aunt said. "As to where it comes from I cannot tell you, but just now, as I was taking off my things, I heard a sweet coo-coo, and looking up I saw this pretty bird perched just outside the window. I stood quite still, for fear of frightening it, and in a few minutes, it flew in here, and then I went and carefully shut the window, that it might not fly away again, whilst I fetched you to see it."

" Is it a wild dove?" Lizzie asked.

" No, I should think not," aunt Atta said, "it probably has escaped from its cage, and flown in here for shelter; see how tame it looks."

" It must be Charlotte's," Lizzie said, " because she was wishing for a dove, and when a stray monkey comes, I'll have it."

" Thank you," aunt Atta said, laughing, "but I don't want the whole Zoological Gardens to escape into my bed room. However you know the pretty dove does not really belong to any of us. We must try to find its owner, and now we will go and see about a cage to put it in."

The children ran after their aunt to tell Mrs. Arden of their pretty visitor, and James was sent off directly to a basket shop near, to buy a wicker cage, and some corn to feed the dove.

Then Mrs. and Miss Arden and all the

children, and Moss and Emma, went into aunt Atta's room to help to catch the dove. But the dove did not seem to want to be caught, and went fluttering about, some of its soft white feathers scattering about, and little Tiny picked them up and stroked her face with them.

"Oh silly dove! we only want to put you in a nice house, and feed you!" Charlotte said, and a minute afterwards the dove came flying down, and lighted on Charlotte's shoulder.

She was too much surprised to catch the dove herself, but aunt 'Atta caught it, and then they all crowded round to see the pretty bird, with its gentle eyes, and soft clean features.

"Poor little thing, how its heart beats!

I must put it into its cage," their aunt said.
She put it inside the large wicker cage,
and then the children were delighted to
watch it picking up some corn and drinking
some water.

"Deedy bird," Tiny at last said indignantly, "it swallows its corn vidout biting
it. Deedy pig!"

Aunt Atta said that doves and pigeons
always did swallow seeds whole, and never
picked them out of the husks, as most other
birds do. At last they left the dove in the
schoolroom and went out for their afternoon
walk ; meanwhile James was to inquire in
the neighbourhood whether any one had lost
a dove, and although the children were half
hoping that nobody would claim it, still
Charlotte could not help thinking how very

sorry whoever had lost it would be, and how glad they would be to know that it was found.

The moment they came home, they all ran to look at the dove, and were delighted to find it so tame as to eat crumbs of bread out of their hands.

When their papa came in, he was taken up to the schoolroom directly, and all the story of the dove was told him by several little voices at once. They could talk of nothing but the dove that evening. The next day however, James brought word that he had found its owner. It belonged to an old gentleman who lived in Wilton Crescent, and who had a good many doves. The children looked rather piteous on hearing this, and Lizzie exclaimed, "If he's got a great many, I'm sure he doesn't want this one back again!"

However it was settled that before Mr. Arden went to his chambers, he should restore the dove to its owner, and Edmund, he said, might go with him. Charlotte looked rather sad, and her mama said, "Take Chatty too, and let her carry the dove—she will take it more tenderly than either you or Edmund."

Edmund looked grand, and said, "Yes, *men* are more rough-fingered than girls"—as if he were quite a man.

Charlotte was very much pleased to go, and soon they set off, she nestling the dove close to her breast, and often kissing its smooth soft head.

They were shewn into a room where old

Mr. Appleby was at breakfast; it opened into a sort of large conservatory, where the children saw some more doves flying about, and heard their cooing.

Mr. Appleby received them very kindly, and thanked the children for taking such care of his dove. He took them into the conservatory, and shewed them all the doves, and told them that up-stairs he had got a large cage full of canaries, and some bulfinches, and two parrots, and a number of other birds; but Charlotte thought that none of those could be half so nice as the doves. He offered to take them to see the other birds, and so Charlotte supposed she must let her dove loose first, but she could not help giving it several kisses first, and the old gentleman saw there were tears in her eyes.

He was a very good-natured old man, and so fond of birds himself that he could quite understand anybody else being so, and he suspected that Charlotte did not like parting with the dove ; so he said,

"You seem very good friends with my little truant, should you like to have him ?"

Charlotte grew very red, and looked at her papa, and Mr. Appleby said,

" I think, as he flew away from me to you, that he must like you better than me, so if you like you shall have him for your own."

" Oh thank you, thank you !" Charlotte exclaimed ; but in a moment she said, "I am afraid, though, he would be happier with his companions, and I should not like to make him unhappy."

" You are a good kind little girl," the old

gentleman said, " and perhaps if he had to live quite alone, he might be dull; but I will pick you out a nice mate for him, and then you will have a pair, and they will coo for you all day long."

Charlotte was quite delighted, and soon a pretty hen dove was caught, and given to Edmund to carry home, and with many thanks to kind Mr. Appleby, they went back.

They were in such a hurry to show their treasures to mama and aunt Atta, and Lizzie and Johnny, and Moss and Emma and Tiny! and Miss Marsh was obliged to stop the lessons, that she might admire the doves also.

They were soon installed in their nice roomy wicker cage, with a well sanded floor, and plenty of corn and hemp seed and water. There was a little cage hanging at one end, which Lizzie called their bed rooom, and she was quite distressed because they would not go to sleep there, but sat all night on their perch.

But Moss put some hay into the little cage, and one morning when Charlotte went to feed the doves, she was enchanted to find a pretty delicate white egg in the middle of the hay. The next morning there was another ; aunt Atta said that pigeons and doves never laid more than two eggs together, so that probably the hen would begin to sit on these directly. So she did, and the children never wearied of watching her brooding so patiently and tenderly over them. At the end of a fortnight, two ugly little birds, with short quills instead of feathers, and great disproportioned heads and beaks, came out of the eggshells. Mr. Arden offended Charlotte very much by calling them the very ugliest little monsters he had ever beheld! Not even mama or aunt Atta could say they thought the little birds pretty; but Charlotte and Lizzie thought them beautiful, and could hardly leave them to go their breakfast.

They had called the parent birds Love-bird and Lady-bird, and now it was an important matter to decide what the young ones were to be called, and the children proposed all sorts of names.

In the evening Charlotte came running to meet her aunt, " Oh aunt Atta, do you know we have quite settled about the little doves! We are going to christen one Apple, after kind old Mr. Appleby, and the other Atta, after you!

" Thank you for the compliment, Chatty dear," her aunt said; "but I do not quite like the way you tell me. Why do you say you will ' christen' the doves? I do not think my Chatty was considering what she said."

" No, aunt, I should not have said so, I know," Charlotte said, colouring.

" Why not?" Johnny asked.

" What does ' christen' mean, Johnny?"

" Why the same thing as baptising, to be sure," Johnny answered.

" Well, and that is a very solemn thing, and one never to be spoken lightly of, or in joke, is it?" aunt Atta said; "and so we should not talk about baptising birds, it sounds irreverent."

" Chatty didn't say *baptise*," Johnny replied; " she said *christen*."

"Well, Johnny, now try and see if you can tell me what to christen means. What is given to little children when they are baptised? When were you called John?" she added, seeing Johnny was puzzled.

"When I was baptised to be sure. Oh, their Christian name, you mean, aunt Atta!" he answered.

"Yes, their Christian name—the name of Christ. So don't you see, darlings, that when you speak of *christening* anybody, you mean giving them the name of Christ, and it is irreverent to speak of that Name, except in a serious, thoughtful manner."

The children all said they should remember and never talk of giving names to things as christening them again.

But Edmund added,—"How many wrong

things grown-up people do! I have often heard people talk of christening their dogs and horses, and all sorts of things. In future, I shall tell them how wicked they are."

"No, Edmund, you must not do that," his aunt said; "it would not be right, it is not your place to be teaching older people. You must be satisfied with correcting yourself of bad habits, and be thankful that GOD has given you friends to teach you what is right and wrong, and not judge other people. If they have never been told about these things, it is not as wrong in them to say them, as it would be in you, who have been told. Now who can tell me a verse out of the Bible, teaching us not to condemn other people?"

"Judge not, that ye be not judged", Johnny answered directly, and Charlotte added

in a moment, "But why dost thou judge
thy brother? or why dost thou set at nought
thy brother? for we shall all stand before
the judgment seat of Christ."   And when
her aunt praised her for being so ready with
the text, she immediately said that Mr.
Brantyre had preached from it a few Sundays
before, when her aunt was ill, and not able
to go to church, and that was why she remembered it, she thought.

Johnny half wondered that Chatty did not
receive the praise without saying anything, but
he saw that aunt Atta seemed more pleased at
Charlotte's not wishing to take more credit
than she deserved, than at her readiness with
a suitable text.

CHAPTER VI.

Great Events.

THE little doves continued in great favor, but something was coming which made the children think less about them.

One morning in June, when they got up, nurse Moss looked very significant and important, and desired the children, as soon as they were dressed, to go away quietly to their aunt's room.

"Why not to mama at once?" Lizzie asked, but Moss only pinched in her lips and smiled, and Chatty said, "Never mind, aunt

Atta will tell us," and they all, except Tiny, went to their aunt's room.

She looked very happy and merry, and as if she had got something pleasant to tell them.

Lizzie was rather put out at not going to her mama's room, and she said somewhat pettishly, " What *is* the matter, aunt? I want to go to mama, and nurse says we mustn't."

" No, not just now," aunt Atta said, " I have got something to shew you first. Do you remember, when you were all settling what animals you should choose, you asked mama what she should like for a pet?"

" Oh, yes," Johnny answered, " and mama said that she had too many of us little two-legged animals to take care of, to want any others."

" Well, but mama has got another little animal in spite of that, do you know !" aunt Atta said.

" Oh what is it? Do tell us, aunt? Is it a dog or a pony? Is it a monkey?"

The last question was Lizzie's.

" Well, Lizzie is nearest right of you all," aunt Atta said, laughing, " but it isn't quite a monkey either. What should you say to a nice plump little baby?"

" Oh, aunt Atta!" they all cried, and looked very much astonished.

"No, but have we really got a baby?" Edmund asked.

" Yes, indeed you have, and a very dear little one too, and you shall see it, if you will promise to be very quiet and not disturb mama, for she is in bed, and we must not make a noise."

"Is it a boy or a girl?" Charlotte asked.

"It is a little boy," aunt Atta answered; "and Mossy says it is just exactly like what Johnny was when he was a baby."

Johnny looked rather scornful at the suggestion that he had ever been a baby; but they all renewed their intreaties to see their new little brother, and so, after again cautioning them to be quiet, aunt Atta took them into the dressing room which adjoined Mrs. Arden's room.

There was a fire, although it was summer, and by the fire stood a pretty little cot of white muslin lined with blue ; near to the cot, holding a tray of tea and bread and butter, stood Mrs. Spearman, whom the children had seen sometimes, and who in a whisper wished them all a very good morning, and hoped they would like their little brother.

"May I take him up, nurse, whilst you take in my sister's breakfast?" aunt Atta said, and the children crowded round her, whilst from under the soft cambric sheets and flannel blankets, she took a little white bundle, from which appeared two wee wee hands, stretching out in all directions, and next a little round face, very red, and with scarcely any eye-brows. All the children were going to cry out, but they remembered their promise to be quiet, so they only whispered their "Oh's!"

The boys said it was the oddest little creature they ever saw, almost as ugly as the dovelets had been. Lizzie, who was still rather discomposed, said she thought it was certainly not a pretty baby; but Charlotte thought it the sweetest, most beautiful little darling that ever was, and begged to fetch Tiny to see it.

Aunt Atta said she might, and Tiny was brought. She seemed too much surprised to laugh, but she put her little fingers into its mouth and its eyes, and touched its hands, (which Edmund declared were not much smaller than her own,) and said, "Tiny a great dal—dis only a baby!" and seemed quite proud of her superior size.

"Does papa know about this new baby?" Johnny asked; "somebody ought to tell him, I think."

Aunt Atta said that he had seen it already, before he went down. Then she said that Charlotte and Edmund might breakfast with their papa and her that morning, as the nurses were rather busier than usual. Poor Lizzie, who had begun what Mossy called a bad day, was still more vexed at her brother and sister breakfasting down stairs, whilst she did not. She had Johnny and Tiny for companions, and they were full of fun and chatter, Johnny telling her, when baby grew old enough to go to school, he should most likely be head-boy, and be able to protect baby, and a great deal more, the fulfilment of which seemed a long way off. But Lizzie could not take any pleasure in their talk, she was getting more and more cross, and Mossy whispered to Emma that she was afraid Miss Lizzie would go on till something brought out one of her passion fits.

"It's a sad pity she's so passionate," Emma said, " for she's a nice little girl."

Aunt Atta was so busy that morning with ordering the house affairs, as Mrs. Arden was not downstairs, and running up and down for her, and talking to the Doctor, and answering several notes that came, that she had no time to spend with the children, and they went as usual to Miss Marsh, who was very kind, and listened with due admiration to their description of the new little brother, without any hair or eyebrows!

Mr. Arden was obliged to go out of town that afternoon, and it was settled that aunt Atta should go to his chambers in the carriage, and take him to the railroad station, so that she might tell him how his wife and his little boy were, the last thing; and they settled together, which Charlotte and Edmund heard, that Moss and Emma should take all the children to the Zoological Gardens, and let them spend a nice long afternoon there.

All this was planned out of kindness and consideration for the children's happiness, and a very nice arrangement it was.

But ill-temper will unfortunately sometimes spoil the pleasantest plans, and so it was in this case. All the morning Lizzie was in "a bad way", she did her lessons with Miss Marsh carelessly, and was ready to be put out of temper every moment.

Aunt Atta and Moss had settled that the children should not walk that morning, in order that they might be quite fresh for their afternoon's expedition; and just because she was not to go out, Lizzie fancied she wanted particularly to go, and was quite angry with Charlotte for not seeming to care.

Lizzie was not at all a greedy child, but owing to the same bad temper, which instead of trying to conquer, she was rather nursing up, she fancied that her dinner was not so nice as usual, and that her aunt had given all the others a better helping than to her. But their aunt was called away before the little ones had finished their dinner, and she desired Charlotte, when all had done, to say grace, and then go into the drawing-room all together.

Generally Lizzie was not jealous of her sister, but as nothing could please her to-day, she was affronted at being left under Charlotte's care; and got up to leave the dining room before grace was said.

"Oh stop a minute, Lizzie," Charlotte said, " I've not said grace."

"I don't care whether you have or not," Lizzie answered crossly; "You're neither mama nor aunt Atta, and I don't see why I'm to be ordered about by you."

"But Lizzie, I don't want to order you about," Charlotte said; "only please stay for grace; you know mama wouldn't like you to go till that was said."

"I'm sure I don't think Lizzie need give herself such airs," Edmund said; "*I'm* not above being said grace for by Charlotte, and I'm ever so much older than Lizzie, and a boy too, which makes a great deal of difference!"

"And I'm a boy too," Johnny cried; "and I like Chatty to say grace, and I'll do all she tells me. I love Chatty, she's always gentle and good-tempered."

Lizzie had left the table already, and now Charlotte having said grace, they all .went upstairs; but her black looks were blacker, and she shook herself impatiently when any of the others spoke to her. Unfortunately, the occupation Lizzie selected for herself was to practise; she had opened the pianoforte, and was just sitting down to it, when her sister came running in from the other drawing-room.

. "Oh please, Lizzie, don't play! Indeed you mustn't! It will disturb mama."

"1 shall though!" Lizzie said very angrily; "you don't suppose your're to be mistress over everything, because mama's ill, do you?" And Lizzie banged her fingers down upon the notes in some not very harmonious chords.

"Oh pray, pray, Lizzie, don't!" cried

Charlotte, very much distressed; " aunt Atta said nobody was to touch this pianoforte, because of mama; it will wake poor mama, indeed it will!" And in great trouble Charlotte took hold of her sister's hands and tried to pull them off the instrument, which she was thumping most discordantly.

By this time, Lizzie's passion had quite gained the upper hand; and getting up, she pushed the music stool violently at Charlotte, who fell down, and then throwing herself upon the floor, began screaming as if she was in dreadful pain. In a moment the door opened, and aunt Atta came in, her bonnet on, and looking quite frightened. Charlotte had got up again, and was trying to go to Lizzie, but she kicked and screamed, and would not let her sister or brothers come near her.

"It's all Lizzie in such a terrible passion!" the boys cried out; "she knocked Chatty over, because she wouldn't let her play to disturb mama, and now she's crying with passion."

Aunt Atta looked quite pale with distress and alarm. "It will make her poor mother so unhappy!" she said.

Aunt Atta had not come into the room alone, though the children were too much engrossed to observe it; Mr. Brantyre, who had been to see their mother, followed her.

"What shall I do?" aunt Atta said to him in perplexity; "the carriage is at the door, and if I wait, I shall make my brother late for the train, but I cannot leave this child in such a state."

"You must go, Esther, directly," Mr.

Brantyre said; "and leave Lizzie to me. I will manage her. Quick, my dear, you are late already—the clock is striking."

Aunt Atta looked very unhappy, but she said, "I believe I must;" and she ran down to the carriage.

Lizzie still lay on the carpet, screaming, she was in too great a passion to see who was near her, and she was very much startled when a stern voice, very unlike aunt Atta's, said peremptorily, "Lizzie, stop screaming this instant."

She looked up, and was terrified and ashamed to see her Godfather, Mr. Brantyre, standing beside her, and witness to her burst of passion. She stopped screaming, however, but did not get up. Mr. Brantyre turned to the other children, who stood by quite frightened at Lizzie's violence, and desired them to go up to Moss, who was waiting to take them to the Zoological Gardens.

"You need not come in here as you go down," he said; "but tell Moss that I will take charge of Lizzie."

Charlotte longed to ask if she might stay with her sister, but she had never seen Mr. Brantyre look so stern, and she did not dare to do anything but obey directly.

When they were gone, Mr. Brantyre looked at Lizzie for a moment, and said very quietly, "When you are more like a little rational being again, Lizzie, you may come and tell me; at present there is no use in speaking to you." And he went to the writing table, and began to write some letters.

Lizzie's violence was over, because she was

frightened, but her passion was not yet con-
quered, and she still lay on the floor, feeling
very angry, and if she had dared, she would
have screamed again, but the tone of voice
in which Mr. Brantyre had said, " Lizzie,
stop screaming this instant," rung in her
ears, and she dare not begin again. She had
heard him mention the Zoological Gardens,
and soon James looked in to say, that the
hackney coach which had been ordered to
take them there, was come. Mr. Brantyre
told James to let Mrs. Moss know, and in a
minute Lizzie heard them all go downstairs,
and soon she heard the carriage drive off.
Then she began to feel herself very much ill-
used, and she cried bitterly. Her Godfather
saw that her tears were at present only anger,
not sorrow, and he took no notice of her.

Presently Lizzie sat up, and looked round. The windows were open, and the scent from the mignonette boxes came very sweetly into the pleasant cheerful room, but every-thing looked very gloomy and wretched to her; and there, when she ventured to peep round at him, sat her Godpapa, whom she had always loved so much, but of whom now she felt so much afraid. Lizzie thought she had never seen anything look so terrible and stern as his high forehead and quiet decided mouth.

Mr. Brantyre did not look up at her, and Lizzie sat on the floor, partly hidden by a large worked table cover, looking at him; and she could not help wishing that she had not given way to her passion, disturbed her poor mama who was ill, made her aunt unhappy, lost her own day's pleasure, and spoiled that of her brothers and sisters, (for she knew they would be thinking of her in disgrace at home), and, worst of all, shewn herself before her Godpapa, whose good opinion she prized almost beyond any one's else, as such a terribly naughty child.

"He never will love me again," Lizzie thought to herself, "he cannot—he will never take me on to his knee and teach me nice things, and call me his dear little girl." Then Lizzie began to cry afresh, but this time it was not in anger.

Mr. Brantyre was well versed in the ways and faults both of grown-up people and little children, and he knew that now Lizzie's passion was over; so he looked up from his writing, but he did not speak.

Then Lizzie crept very slowly towards him, and thought she would say: "I am very—very sorry"—but when she tried to speak the words were choked, and she could only sob.

"If you are going to try and be good, Lizzie," Mr. Brantyre said, "come to me, and try to stop crying."

She shewed that she did want to be good, for she came quite up to Mr. Brantyre, and put her face down on his knee, and tried to stop her sobs, but she could not quite.

He did not offer to take her up, or to pet her in any way, but said very quietly, "When you are fit to listen to me, Lizzie, I have something to say to you."

Poor Lizzie tried to gulp down the lump in her throat, and at last she managed to say, "I am so sorry that I am such a naughty girl!" and then, though she bit her lips and tried to stop, the crying would begin again.

Mr. Brantyre put his hand kindly upon her shoulder, for he saw that she was trying to stop her tears, and said, " Well, now then, Lizzie, I must shew you how very very sad it is for a little girl who has been baptised and taught as you have been, to give way to these bad passions. Tell me Whose child you were made, when you were brought as a little baby into the Church to be baptised?"

" GOD'S", Lizzie answered.

"And as His child, you promised to do His works, and serve and please Him, and to renounce the works of the devil. Now tell me, Lizzie, are ill-temper and passion the works of GOD or of Satan?"

"Of Satan"—Lizzie answered in a very low voice.

"Then, although you are GOD's child, and have promised to do His works, you have been breaking your promise and doing Satan's work instead."

Lizzie drew a long sigh, and looked very unhappy; she did not venture to look up in Mr. Brantyre's face, for she knew that it was grave and sad.

"I am very sorry," she said at last, with an effort not to begin sobbing again; "Will you forgive me, and not be very angry, please?"

"But who is it that you have displeased most?" her Godfather asked. "You have behaved unkindly and wrongly to your mama, and to your brothers and sisters, and to all about you, but there is One besides, Whom you have displeased most of all. Who gave you a good mama, and told you to love and honour her? and Who gave you brothers and sisters to love and agree with?"

" God," Lizzie again said.

" Yes, and He is displeased and grieved when you forget His Will, and give yourself up to do what is wicked."

"I cannot help being passionate," Lizzie said at last, and she felt quite frightened at her own boldness in speaking so to Mr. Brantyre. "I want not to be, but something within does get so very angry, and then I can't help getting into a passion; I wish I could, it makes me very unhappy;

mama and aunt Atta, and Moss and Chatty, and everybody will dislike me, and you will never love me again I know," and the tears could not be kept in any longer.

Mr. Brantyre was satisfied that Lizzie was thoroughly penitent now, so he took the little girl on to his knee, and his face looked less severe, as he said, " I cannot let Lizzie say she *cannot help* being passionate ; it is very difficult I know, and alone, you cannot help it, but if you really wish to cure your temper it may be done. It is my duty, both as your Priest and your Godfather, to help you to cure it. Shall I help you, Lizzie?"

Poor Lizzie felt quite comforted at his voice, it sounded so different from what it had done, and she rested her head, which ached with sobbing, against his arm.

" Well now," he said, " tell me just what happened to-day. Try and be very honest, and don't make any excuses for yourself, and see if you can remember when you began to get angry, and how much you tried to check your ill-temper."

This was rather a hard thing for Lizzie to do, but she was a truthful little girl, and she did try to tell Mr. Brantyre exactly the truth, beginning at her feeling disappointed not to go into her mama's room, and going on all through her crossness with the other children and Miss Marsh, and her ill-temper at dinner, and then the sad burst of passion in which her Godpapa had found her.

He helped her sometimes in her story, and she could not help wondering how well he seemed to understand all she had been thinking and doing—better than she did herself. And when it was all told, Lizzie felt much easier, and she was not so afraid to look up in Mr. Brantyre's face.

" I think you have told me everything very honestly," he said, when she had quite finished her little tale, " and now you must answer me a few questions as honestly. Is this the first time you have been in one of these great passions?"

" No," Lizzie said.

" And have you not been fully told how wrong they are, and how displeasing to God?"

" Yes."

" Now tell me, if I had been in the room, do you think that you should have given way to that sad fit of passion?"

" No," Lizzie thought not.

"Or if you knew I had been watching you all the morning at your lessons, and with your brothers and sisters, should you have gone on just as you did?"

"No."

"Why not, Lizzie?"

"Because—why because I should have been afraid."

"Afraid of what?"

"Of making you angry, and of your not loving me any more."

"Was any one watching you all the morning, Lizzie?" Mr. Brantyre said very gravely.

"Aunt Atta was scarcely down stairs at all;" the little girl said at first, but in a moment she added, "I know what you mean—GOD was watching me."

"Yes," her Godfather said, "He saw

you, and not only saw you look cross, and
heard you speak angrily and improperly,
which is all I should have seen, but He saw
the angry, irritable thoughts, rising in your
heart, and He saw—which I could not have
seen—exactly how much effort you made
to stop the passionate feelings from growing
stronger, or whether you indulged them and
let them have their way. Did you think
of this?

"No," Lizzie said mournfully.

"But you think, Lizzie, that if you were
always near me, and saw me watching you,
that would prevent you from ever having
these fits of passion, and that partly because
you love me, and partly because you fear me?
Well now, do you not think that if you
remembered that the Holy Angels are always

around us, although we cannot see them, and more than that, that GOD Himself is always watching you, and sees and hears everything, however little, that you do, would not remembering *that* help you quite as much, and more too? because, though I believe you do love me very much, you owe a great deal more love to GOD, and though you may fear seeing me look displeased, His displeasure is very much more serious, for those who die with it still resting on them, will be miserable and unhappy for all eternity."

"But I can see you when you are by, or mama, or aunt Atta," Lizzie said, "and that makes me remember; but I can't see GOD or the Angels, and so I forget that They are there."

" Yes, that is what we all do when we are sinning," Mr. Brantyre said; "if we really believed and remembered that we are never from under His All-Seeing Eyes, we should be much more careful not to do wrong. But, Lizzie, I said I would help you to learn to remember. Now, whenever you feel a naughty passionate thought coming up in your little heart, try to run away, upstairs into the nursery, or into the other drawing-room, or anywhere where you can be alone for a few minutes, and ask yourself whether you were recollecting that GOD and His holy Angels saw you, and saw the angry thought or cross word? and then kneel down and say a little prayer to GOD to keep you from displeasing Him, and to keep you in mind of the promises you gave when you were made

His child; and by that time I think the naughty feeling will be nearly gone, and every time you do this, you will make your victory easier. Will you try?"

" Yes, indeed," Lizzie said.

" You will not conquer all at once, you know. Grown-up people, and very good people too, all have to keep on constantly fighting, and trying to keep down bad thoughts and tempers, and unless they pray to GOD to help them, they will not succeed any better than a little girl like you. And then you shall tell me sometimes how you are getting on, and I shall ask GOD too, to help you, and keep you in remembrance of Him. There is another way too," Mr. Brantyre went on, " of helping people to remember not to do wrong. When you were a very little child,

Lizzie, you once put your finger into the candle-flame, and scorched it.   Do you recollect that?"

"Oh yes!" Lizzie said, "and it hurt so much that I used to cry whenever I saw a taper afterwards, and it was a long time before I liked to touch one; mama always sent one of the others to light her tapers."

"Well, just as remembering the pain which you felt kept you from putting your hand into the candle-flame again, so suffering pain is the consequence of doing wrong, and keeps people from doing the same thing again, and bringing fresh pain upon themselves.   This is the use of punishment.   Can you understand that, Lizzie?"

Lizzie nodded her head.

"Then you see, in order to help you to

remember what you have done wrong, and the pain of it, you must be punished; not because I am angry with you, but because I love you, and wish to help you to remember to fight against your ill-temper, and cure it. Do you not think that is right?"

Lizzie thought it was, though she wished it was not.

"Perhaps if there is nothing to help you to remember, you may soon forget all about to-day, and about your resolutions to try and cure your passionate temper; but if you suffer pain in consequence, real pain, you will recollect it, just as you still recollect burning your finger, and so keep away from fire."

Lizzie looked rather disconsolate. Her Godfather soon said, "I am sure that as soon as your aunt and brothers and sisters come home, you will tell them how sorry you are for having been naughty and grieved them. And then we must think of some real punishment that will help you to remember to-day. I think mama had promised that aunt Atta should bring you all to my school-children's feast next week, did she not?"

"Yes," Lizzie said, and they had all been counting it as one of their great pleasures. Chatty and Edmund and Johnny had been last summer, but she had never been, she was with aunt Emily when it took place.

"Well then," her Godfather said, "I think if you lose that pleasure for another year, it will help you to remember about trying not to be passionate, and so we will settle that. You shall stay away this year; and next year,

if you have become much less passionate,
I am sure you will not regret having lost
the pleasure this time, though now it seems
very hard—I want it to seem very hard," he
added, seeing that Lizzie's eyes were fast
filling with tears.

"I will try and remember, indeed I will,"
she said; and then added in a whisper,
"Are you displeased with me still? Will
you ever call me your dear little child
again?"

"My dear, very dear child!" Mr. Brantyre
said kindly, and then he put his hand on
Lizzie's curly head, and asked GOD to bless
her and keep her His child.

Aunt Atta came home just afterwards,
and when she saw that Lizzie was sitting
on her Godfather's knee, and looked quite

good, although her eyes were still red and swelled with crying, she was very glad.

Mr. Brantyre told her some of what they had been saying, and aunt Atta promised that she too would help Lizzie to try and conquer her temper. She was very sorry for Lizzie not to go to the School-feast, next week, but she thought it quite worth the pain, if it helped her to remember.

Then Mr. Brantyre went away, and Lizzie went upstairs with her aunt to see baby; and as her mama was awake, aunt Atta took her in to her for a few minutes. Her mama kissed her, and asked how she liked the baby; and then Lizzie whispered, "I was very naughty, and screamed, and was in a great great passion, mama; did I disturb you? But I'm quite good now, and Mr. Brantyre and aunt Atta are going to help me never to be in another."

But Mrs. Spearman said, that Lizzie must not stay and talk to her mama; so she went back to the drawing-room, and sat very quietly by her aunt, who had some letters to write; and as Lizzie worked at a little bag in cross stitch which she was making for Moss, she thought about all that had happened, and what Mr. Brantyre had said, and how very *very* sorry she should be not to go to the school-children's feast; and Chatty would be so sorry too, she knew.

When the bell for evensong began to ring, aunt Atta shut up her desk, and prepared to go for her bonnet. She saw Lizzie looking at her rather wistfully, and then she said, " Do you think, Lizzie, that if

I took you to church with me, you should be very attentive, and try to ask GOD again to forgive you for having been naughty?"

Lizzie was quite pleased at this, and she ran quickly into the nursery, and brought her bonnet and spencer to her aunt, who put them on for her, and took Lizzie with her.

The little girl knelt very quietly by her aunt, and when she repeated, "We have left undone those things which we ought to have done, and we have done those things which we ought not to have done," after Mr. Brantyre, she remembered all that *she* had done "which she ought not to have done", that day, and hoped GOD would forgive her.

The other children did not come back from the Zoological Gardens till past six o'clock; and though Lizzie felt rather ashamed to meet them, she ran in a great hurry to kiss them all, and Mossy too, and say she was very sorry for having been so cross. They all kissed her, and began directly to tell her about what they had seen and done. Lizzie was quieter than usual at tea, but afterwards she went with Charlotte into aunt Atta's room, and sat by the open window, watching the bright evening sun on the Church tower, and told her a great deal about what had happened, and what Mr. Brantyre had said, and how she was not to go to the School-feast, to help her to remember. Charlotte could hardly help crying, to think of her sister's trouble, and she said she did hope Mr. Brantyre would never be very angry with her, for she should be so frightened she should never stop crying!

Soon Emma came to call Lizzie to go to bed, and she jumped up, and ran away immediately; and Charlotte and the boys were glad to follow early, for they were quite tired, with their long day's amusement.

But before they went to bed, Charlotte reminded the others that now they must pray for the new baby, as well as all the other people, whom they named in their prayers, and as for the present they could not give it any name, (for it was not baptised), they agreed to call it "little brother."

So from that evening all the children asked GOD to bless and keep their little baby brother.

When aunt Atta told their mama, the tears came into her eyes, though she smiled

and looked pleased; and she and aunt Atta
prayed too, for him, and for all their dear
little ones.

CHAPTER VII.

The Christening.

IT was not very long before Mrs. Arden was able to have the children in and out of her room a good deal, though still aunt Atta made their papa's breakfast, and wrote all the notes, and took the children out, and heard the lessons which their mama generally heard.

They liked very much being in her room, and fetching anything she wanted, and telling her all their little plans and pleasures that went on, and she was always glad to hear that Miss Marsh and aunt Atta and Moss said that they were good.

One day, when they were admiring baby, (for by this time, even Edmund and Johnny thought him very pretty), their mama told them that it was settled that he should be baptised the next day, Thursday, for he would be a fortnight old that day, and it was the very day on which aunt Atta, who was to be his Godmother, had been baptised. Then came a great many questions about his sponsors, and his name. Mrs. Arden said they had agreed to call him Walter, which was the name of her father, who was dead, and of the children's uncle, Sir Walter Melton. He would be one of baby's Godfathers, and Mr. Temple, a friend of their papa's and a clergyman, would be the other.

All the children liked the name Walter, and they began to try and remember all the well-known people who had been called by that name. Johnny recollected Sir Walter Tyrell, who shot William Rufus; he liked him for doing that, though Chatty said that if he had not done it by accident, as she believed he did, she should think it was very wicked of him, although certainly it was a good thing for that bad King to be taken away from oppressing the poor people. Edmund said there was Sir Walter Manny, King Edward III's knight, who was so brave that his royal master fought under his banner in France; and Wat Tyler; but Charlotte objected to their little Walter being compared to the insolent rebel, whom the Lord Mayor, Walworth, killed, because he lifted his sword against the young King, Richard II. Lizzie made them all laugh, by saying, what a pity it was that baby's name was not to be William, because then they could have found so many more historical personages to liken him to. As it was, they could not remember any one else till they came to Sir Walter Raleigh, and Lizzie stopped to tell the story of his throwing his cloak in the mud for Queen Elizabeth to walk on, to Tiny, who clapped her hands, and then Johnny spread one of his mama's shawls on the floor, and handed Tiny most gallantly over it, declaring that she was Queen Elizabeth, and he was Sir Walter Raleigh.

Charlotte said, that of all the Walters there was none she liked half so much as Sir Walter Scott, who wrote their favourite

"Tales of a Grandfather," and her darling little "Lay of the Last Minstrel," which aunt Atta gave her on her last birthday.

Mrs. Arden asked aunt Atta whether there had ever been any Saint Walter, as they had got so many knights of the name; and she said that there had been a Saint Walter, a very holy man, who lived in Italy, in the 13th century, and was greatly venerated for his humility and excellence, and that she believed that there had also lived an Englishman, of the same name, who was canonized, and also a French Abbot, much honoured by King Philip the first of France.

So it was agreed that their little Walter should be as good as these holy men, and as brave as Sir Walter Manny and Sir Walter Raleigh, and as agreeable and talented as

Sir Walter Scott, which satisfied all parties. Meanwhile the little gentleman himself, lay sleeping very quietly in his mama's arms, not at all aware how much he was the topic of conversation in the family.

That evening Charlotte and Lizzie were sitting in their mama's room working; the boys had gone out with their papa, and aunt Atta was playing with Tiny in the drawing-room. The little girls sat very quietly, and Mrs. Arden noticed that though Lizzie talked away to her sister, Charlotte answered very little, and seemed to be thinking about something else. At last she inquired what made Chatty so thoughtful.

"Shall I tell you, mama?" she said; "no, you will think me very silly, I'm afraid. I think I will, too. You know we walked with Alice Eaton in the Park this afternoon, and we told her all about our baby and its Baptism, and she said that she wondered that you and papa liked to have just a common Christening like that; and then she told us about the grand Christening her uncle had last week for his little girl; how she was baptised in Lord Morton's own house in the evening, and there were a great many very smart people, all beautifully dressed, and the baby's frock was white satin and lace, and then after the Christening there was a very large party and a ball, and all sorts of things, and Alice was at it all, and sat up till nearly one o'clock in the morning!"

"And do you want papa and me to imitate these fine doings, and let you and Lizzie sit up till one o'clock; is that what my little Chatty was thinking about?" Mrs. Arden asked.

"No, not exactly, mama," Charlotte said, hesitating, "but I couldn't help thinking it must have been rather nice too."

"What was rather nice, dear, the ball, or the baby's frock, or the Baptism?"

"Oh mama, I know what you mean! you mean that the Baptism itself is of too much consequence for those other things to matter; but still, I should like to have a grand Christening, I do think!"

"Shall we send to Mr. Brantyre, and ask him to come and baptise baby up here to-morrow?" Mrs. Arden asked; "and say that we think it looks grander than taking him to God's House, and to the Font, where other babes are baptised, and made God's children?"

"Oh, mama!" Charlotte exclaimed, "you are joking! I don't think Mr. Brantyre would do it unless baby was ill."

"I think so too," Mrs. Arden said; "he would probably tell us to look in our Prayer books for the office of Private Baptism, and desire us to observe that it is said there that children are not to be baptised at home *without great cause and necessity,* and I do not think we could quite plead that. Besides, Charlotte, do you know I think our Christening will really be a much grander one than this of little Lady Julia Eaton, which you have heard so much of. You say that she was baptised in her father's beautiful house—but our baby will be baptised in GOD's Own House, the place where He has promised always to be; and if there were a great many smart people present at that Christening, why, at our's I hope we shall have a very reverent and earnest congregation, who will pray heartily for dear baby; and a mighty Company of GOD'S Holy Angels, who are always in His House, ready to carry the prayers of His people up to Him. And I think we are all more likely to remember what a very great thing is being done for our little darling, in our own beautiful Church, at the Font, in the midst of prayer, than we should in the midst of a large evening party. There would be something that would rather grate upon my feelings in that, Charlotte, and would seem to me inconsistent. Can you tell me, dear, what there is in such a conclusion to the day which would be out of keeping with the promises baby had just been making?" Charlotte thought a few minutes, and then said,—

"I think you mean, mama, that he will promise to renounce the vain pomp and glory of the world, and that the large party and fine clothes would be a sort of contradiction to that."

"Yes, that is what I meant," Mrs. Arden answered. "I should be sorry to appear even to think such things of more consequence than the Holy Sacrament with which I hope our precious baby will be blessed; and I think that the closer we keep to the arrangements made for it by the Church, the better. But I should quite wish that the day, which is so important to him, should be more than a common day to you; and that you should enjoy it particularly.—Mr. Brantyre and Mr. Temple and uncle Walter and aunt Emily have all promised to come here after the Baptism, and as I should not be strong enough to go down to dinner with them, they will come up here to tea with me, and you shall all sit up and have tea with us here. Shall you like that?"

" Oh yes, very much indeed!" both the little girls said, and Lizzie added, " And then Chatty, the next time you see Alice Eaton, you can tell her how wrong it is to make such a to-do about a Christening, and how much better our's is than her little cousin's."

" No," Mrs. Arden said, " Charlotte must not do that, Lizzie, it is not either her place or mine, to judge what other people should do.

We are quite certain what *we* ought to do, and then we have no excuse if we do not do it; but we must not set ourselves up above other persons and fancy ourselves much better than they are, or all the while we shall be making a terrible mistake; for there are few greater faults than self-conceit and self-satisfaction.

"But now, my children, I must get a little rest before papa comes home; so run down to aunt Atta, and tell her I think my Tiny should be going to bed."

The next day came, a bright beautiful summer's day, on which baby was for the first time to leave his room, and be taken to church to be made a Christian.

Charlotte and Edmund quite remembered Tiny's Christening, and Johnny and Lizzie

had often been present during the Baptismal
service on Sunday afternoons, but they had
never been part of the christening party
before, and to-day they were to be quite close
to the font. Charlotte was particularly
pleased at Tiny's being allowed to go; and as
her mama would not be there, and aunt Atta
was to hold baby, it was settled that Charlotte
should take charge of her little sister : a
dignity which made her feel very important,
and very anxious to behave as attentively
and thoughtfully as mama or aunt Atta
could do.

All the children went to see baby dressed
in his nice white robe and cap, and Lizzie
said she thought Mr. Brantyre would not be
able to help kissing him, when he had him in
his arms; he looked so sweet. Their house

was so near the church that there was no need of the carriage; and a little before five they all went in a sort of procession; Mr. Arden and aunt Atta; uncle Walter and aunt Emily; Mrs. Temple and all the children; Moss, who carried baby; and Emma; and Mrs. Drew, the housekeeper; who had been at their own mama's christening, and said she wouldn't miss going to baby's for anything.

They all took their places near the Font, and though at first the new position rather distracted the children, they all tried to remember where they were, and Who saw them; and Lizzie thought, too, how important it was that Tiny should have a good example in her brothers and sisters. Now and then she just peeped back to see whether baby was asleep, and there he lay in nurse's arms, looking so placid and sweet and still.

When Mr. Brantyre, and his Curate, Mr, Archer, came to the Font, Lizzie fixed her eyes on them, and scarcely stirred till she saw nurse take off baby's mantle and cap, and then give him to aunt Atta, who put him very gently into Mr. Brantyre's arms. Tiny was very good, and never spoke once; for she quite understood that she was in GOD's House, and that her little brother was being given to Mr. Brantyre that he might come back to them, made a holy little child.

Mrs. Arden had watched the party going to church, and as they came back the children saw her at the window, and they ran as fast as they could up to her room, to tell her how nicely Tiny had behaved, and how good

Walter had been, and how very dear he looked when Mr. Brantyre held him over the Font, and how he did not cry at all, but only stretched out his little waxy fingers, and looked as if he wanted to stroke the Priest's face. Tiny too had her own account of the matter to give to her mama; and she said, "Tiny twite a big dal now, for Tiny do to church, and be so dood there!"

There was a very merry tea party in Mrs. Arden's room that evening. Charlotte helped aunt Atta to make the tea, and Edmund, Johnny, and Lizzie waited upon everybody; and it was actually past nine o'clock before they went to bed! When Charlotte and Lizzie knelt down to say their prayers, they did not forget a little bit of quiet talk they had had with Mr. Brantyre, who told them to think over what had been promised that day for baby Walter, and to remember that the same promises had been made for them, which they were bound to fulfil.

CHAPTER VIII.

A Change to the Country.

"MASTER Edmund, you should not speak so! indeed you should not!" nurse Moss was saying just as aunt Atta came for the children, who were going out for a walk. "It's very wrong to make a joke about anything serious, and I'm sure your aunt will say so too."

Edmund looked rather ashamed, as he turned round and saw his aunt, and Johnny cried out, "Oh, aunt Atta, do you know what Edmund said, it was so funny! He said—"

"Stop, Johnny dear," aunt Atta interrupted; "from what Mossy says, I think Edmund must have been making some silly jest, which it was wrong in him to make, and would be just as wrong in you to repeat. I would rather not hear it."

Both Edmund and Johnny were silent; and as soon as they got into the Square, where they were going instead of the Park, as it was very hot, aunt Atta said, "I have been meaning to tell you what I think about some of those things I have heard you say lately, Edmund, which perhaps you have hardly thought of as wrong, but which I am sure you will soon see cannot be right. I heard you ask Johnny a riddle yesterday, which was on some sacred subject; and once or twice in your play I have heard you use Scripture words. I'm sure, Edmund dear, you did not mean to be irreverent; but those sort of sayings are very irreverent and disrespectful to God."

"Oh aunt Atta!" Edmund said, "I hope I am not irreverent. I'm sure I never thought so!"

"No, dear," his aunt answered; "I think you have said the things I allude to out of mere thoughtlessness; but people soon acquire a habit of any kind, and few are more easily caught than that of introducing holy words into common conversation, and making jokes about sacred things. You would not think it right to laugh in Church, would you, Edmund?"

"Oh, aunt Atta, of course not!"

" But if you have heard some droll saying in connexion either with a text in the Bible, or with any passage in the Service, it might be very difficult to you to help smiling, when the subject was brought before your mind in Church.   I have known people disturbed and troubled all their life through by some foolish saying which had amused them about some sacred subject, or the recollection of some absurd accident, with which they could not help associating it. If persons would think of this, they would be more particular I am sure, and not give way to the temptation of saying something witty or amusing about solemn things to make others laugh; they would remember it is irreverent, and that would check the joking thought directly."

" It almost seems," Charlotte said, " as if

the third Commandment meant that, by saying, 'Thou shalt not take the Name of the Lord thy GOD in vain.' "

" Yes, Chatty, I think it does; because those sort of sayings and jokes are in vain, that is, they are for no good, but only meant to make people laugh, which we all feel we should not do about anything sacred."

" I think, aunt," Johnny began, " that Mrs. Wyatt takes GOD's Name in vain; for when she comes to see mama, her talk is all so stuffed with texts and bits of hymns, that it quite makes me laugh ! "

" I dare say Mrs. Wyatt means to be very reverential," aunt Atta answered, " but it is certainly much better to avoid that way of speaking, and never use the Holy Name of GOD, or talk of anything religious, without thinking what we are going to say, and whether we are justified in doing so—and not for our own sakes only, but for other people's, as they are often influenced by the things we say thoughtlessly.   There is a passage in the book I brought out to read whilst you ran about, which seems written on purpose for us.   Here it is.   It was written by Dr. Fuller, who lived in the unfortunate times when England was dis-tracted by civil war between the Royalists and Puritans.   Dr. Fuller was a Priest, and Chaplain to Princess Henrietta, King Charles the First's daughter.   So you can see why he called this quaint little book 'Good Thoughts in Bad Times.'   Now listen to what Fuller says about bad jests.   'Almost twenty years since, I heard a profane jest, and still re-

member it.   How many pious passages of far
later date have I forgotten! It seems my
soul is like a filthy pond, wherein fish die
soon, and frogs live long.   Lord, raze this
profane jest out of my memory. `Leave not
a letter thereof behind, lest my corruption
(an apt scholar) guess it out again; and be
pleased to write some pious meditation in the
place thereof.   And grant, Lord, for the
time to come (because such bad guests are
easier kept out) that I may be careful not to
admit what I find so difficult to expel'."

"How very nice," Charlotte said; "I like
that, aunt Atta, very much, and we will all
remember it, and never say anything lightly
about religious things.   Mossy often tells us
that text from S. James, about 'the tongue
is a little member, and boasteth great things.

Behold how great a matter a little fire kindleth'."

" Yes," her aunt replied, " if we could always remember that, and stop the angry or foolish, or untrue words that rise to our lips, it would save us from many a sinful action.   And now let me go on with my old friend Dr. Fuller, whilst you have a good game.   I see Emma and Tiny at the gate. Edmund, will you run with the key and let them in?"

Not many days after this, Johnny came in from his walk complaining that his head ached, and his eyes smarted so, he could not eat any dinner, and laid down on the carpet in a cool corner of the room seeming very uncomfortable.   Mrs. Arden sent directly for advice, and when Dr. Head came, he said that Johnny was sickening with the measles. Mrs. Arden was very much distressed at hearing this, for she did not like her little baby to catch the infection, and as she had never had the complaint herself, she felt afraid that she might be ill, and unable to be of any use in nursing her children. When Mr. Arden came home and saw Dr. Head, he decided that there was no doubt as to what should be done. Mrs. Arden, and the children who were not infected must go to her brother's, Sir Walter Melton's, as he had no children to whom the measles could be carried, and Johnny was to remain at home with Moss and aunt Atta, who had had the complaint, and was quite ready to be nurse. Mrs. Arden would not at first hear of leaving her child, but when the doctor and her husband shewed her how desirable it was that her little ones should not take the measles, she consented for their sakes to go to her brother's. That very evening Edmund and Lizzie shewed symptoms of the measles, and as it was thought that Charlotte could not escape, she having been constantly with the others, only Tiny and Walter went away with their mama.

So now aunt Atta became a regular sick nurse. For a few days all the children were very uncomfortable and feverish; but Johnny soon began to get better, and then Edmund, and then Lizzie, and there was no reason to be uneasy about them. Charlotte however, who was not taken ill for several days later, was much worse; she had a great deal of fever, and for two nights her aunt sat up with her, trying to keep her cool and quiet.

Aunt Atta could not help feeling very anxious about her, and much more so because her mama was absent; but she knew that all in her power to relieve the little girl was done, and she trusted to GOD to do that which was best, in making her better or not.

At last the complaint took a good turn; the fever went away, and Dr. Head said Charlotte was doing quite well. But she was very weak and uncomfortable, and still required a great deal of care. Aunt Atta had her little bed in her own room, and she nursed her, and fed her, and amused her by reading aloud, and telling her stories, and Charlotte was almost envied by the other children who did not require so much of their aunt's attention.

One day aunt Atta proposed to Charlotte to write to her mama, who had not seen her since the beginning of her illness, although she heard every day most minutely all that was going on. So, as Charlotte lay on her aunt's sofa, she wrote :—

"My dearest mama—I am getting a great deal better. I sleep in aunt Atta's room and she reads to me. She has read *Amy Herbert* and several other books. The doves are brought in every day, and I like to hear them coo. Edmund and Johnny and Lizzie go out now in the square with Mossy; they are nearly quite well. I am so glad that you and Tiny and baby did not have the measles. When you do have them, Lizzie and I can nurse you, as we have had them. Give my love to uncle Walter and aunt Emily.

Your very affectionate daughter,

CHARLOTTE ARDEN."

In reply to this, Charlotte received a nice long letter from her mama, telling her that papa had taken a place in the country, and that very soon he and aunt Atta would take the four eldest children there, and then as soon as the doctor thought there was no fear of the little ones taking the measles, she should come to join them with Tiny and Walter.

This was very good news, and all the children had many questions to ask about Eston Manor, the place Mr. Arden had taken.   It was in Hampshire, not very far from the railroad, he said, and it was a nice place with a large garden, where they might play and run about famously.

Lizzie thought the day fixed for their removal would never come; but it did come at last, and they all drove to the railway station, and soon were seated in a carriage, steaming off to Winchester, where they were to leave the train and go on in two carriages to Eston Manor. They were pleased to find a large cheerful-looking house, with some fine trees, and a very pretty lawn and garden. There were thick shady woods and a nice heath-covered common too, close to the house, and the children looked for many a pleasant walk.

A very few days afterwards, Mrs. Arden and her little ones joined them, and then they thought all would be quite perfect.

All except Charlotte had quite recovered from their illness—she was not ill, but still she was rather weak, and all the care and indulgence she had had, made her a little more fretful than usual. She was naturally rather a shy timid child, somewhat inclined to be low-spirited, and now she appeared less ready than usual to struggle against her fretfulness.

Mrs. Arden soon saw that a very little contradiction made Charlotte unhappy, and though she was not actually out of temper, she would go and cry and complain in a peevish manner.

Mrs. Arden and aunt Atta agreed that the best possible thing was for Charlotte to return gradually to her usual occupations, and aunt Atta undertook to be governess. She found, however, that of all the children, Charlotte was the least ready to settle to anything, and her little easy lessons, for they began very gently, seemed quite a burden to her. If aunt Atta read aloud any amusing story, Charlotte liked it, but if nothing was done to amuse her, she would dawdle about unoccupied, and was of course very dull in consequence. Neither children nor grown-up people can be happy when they are wasting the time which GOD has given us that we may use it for our own good, and that of our neighbours. Even young children are responsible for their use of time, according to what they have learnt to do, as they may both improve themselves and help others; but of course, older people are still more so.

One day, Mrs. Arden had promised, if it was fine, she would drive with the children to spend the afternoon with a friend of hers in the neighbourhood, who had a very pretty vicarage and garden. They knew and liked Mrs. Charlton, so that the expedition promised to be very agreeable, and they looked to it with great pleasure. But it is an old story, for pleasant plans to be defeated by causes which we cannot help, and so it was in this case. The bright sunny morning clouded in, and by the children's dinner-time, the small soft rain had set in, which bid fair to continue for the rest of the day: there was no hope of a drive that afternoon.

It was quite natural that the children should feel disappointed, and their mama and aunt both said they were very sorry, but that the pleasure would be in store for another day, and they must try and make themselves happy at home.

Lizzie's face had clouded a little at first, but she had been much more watchful over her temper since the day on which Walter was born, when she had been so passionate; and she eat her currant tart in silence—for fear she should say anything cross.   Her mama noticed this, and saw why Lizzie was so quiet, and she felt very much pleased to see how her little girl was improving.

When dinner was over, Lizzie jumped up quite good-naturedly, and proposed a good noisy game, which she always enjoyed very much, and they all ran off to a large billiard room, where they could play as noisily as they pleased without disturbing anybody.

Tiny did not like rough plays, but she got a large book of pictures, and Edmund lifted her up on to the billiard table, and there she sat, quite happy with her book, and watching the others play.

Aunt Atta went to her own room for a little while, and then she went to the drawing-room. Mrs. Arden was up in the nursery with baby, so there was no one there but Charlotte, who lay stretched in an arm-chair near the window, with a melancholy face, and seemingly no occupation, but watching the rain as it soaked into the turf before the windows.

" Chatty dear! " her aunt said in surprise, " I thought you were with the others! "

" I didn't want to play," Charlotte said in a sorrowful voice, " I don't like play—it tires me so."

" And so you came to sit here," aunt Atta said; " but you do not look very cheerful,. my child! What are you doing to amuse yourself? "

"Nothing," Charlotte said, "I do not like—I havn't got anything to do. It is so dull! I wanted so much to go to Mrs. Charlton's!"

"So we all did," aunt Atta said, "but you see that was settled for us, so I think the best thing we can do is to be busy and happy at home. I have been writing two letters, and now I am going to copy some music for Miss Hamilton—what are you going to do?"

"I don't know," Charlotte again said in a doleful tone.

Her aunt prepared her music and sat down to it, writing busily. Charlotte continued a few minutes in the great arm-chair, then she got up and walked to the window, and stood looking out on the wet prospect

before her, which certainly was not very
cheering. Then with a heavy sigh, she
moved off to a table where Johnny had left
his tee-totum, and spun that once or twice,
but not as if she found any particular
amusement in it.   At last she came to a sofa
which was near her aunt, and threw herself
upon it, exclaiming, "Oh! dear dear, how
wretched bad weather makes one!"

"I am sorry that it makes you wretched,
Chatty," aunt Atta said; "I think fine
weather much pleasanter, but the rain does
not make me wretched."

"No, but then you're grown up, aunt
Atta, and can do what you like, and employ
yourself pleasantly."

"It does not follow," aunt Atta said,
smiling, "that I always particularly *like*

what I do; for instance, Chatty, I do most exceedingly dislike copying music, I assure you; but as Miss Hamilton wants these songs it would not be kind if I did not copy them."

" Well but, aunt Atta, you see it is quite different for a grown-up person to do disagreeable things, and a little girl, don't you think so?"

" I think, Charlotte, that everybody has a certain quantity of disagreeable things to do; and that the people who set about them most in earnest, and also who earliest are accustomed just to do what is right, whether it is agreeable or disagreeable, are generally the happiest, and made least uncomfortable.   However, I think you have imposed one of the most disagreeable of all things upon yourself lately; this afternoon for instance."

" What do you mean, aunt Atta? I'm sure I want to be happy and amused, only somehow I'm very dull. What disagreeable thing am I about?"

" The worst of all, dear—doing nothing."

" I don't seem to care for anything," Charlotte again said.

" No, you have got into unsettled do-nothing ways in your illness, and now it is a greater effort than you like to make, to become busy and active again. But I am sure, dear, that you will not be happy whilst you give way to indolence; you have two very sufficient causes for discontent; want of occupation, and an inward feeling that you are not doing right; for I am sure my Chatty knows that it is not quite right to waste time in dawdling about and complaining, does she not?"

" Yes, aunt Atta," Charlotte said colouring; " I am afraid it isn't right to be discontented, but really I cannot help it."

" And I think you could, if you tried," aunt Atta said.

" I should like to try!" Charlotte began; "but everything seems a trouble. Now tell me, aunt Atta, how would you have me begin."

" I would have you begin this very moment," aunt Atta said, " by picking up that sofa cushion which you threw down just now; and then you might put those books straight, and wheel the arm-chair into its place, instead of leaving it out in the middle of the room. You know it is all in keeping with the old maiden aunt's character to like a tidy room ! And then, Chatty, I think you might run up to mama, and ask her, whether, this damp chilly afternoon, it would not be well to light the fire."

All these little offices were executed in a few minutes, and Charlotte quite brightened up, as she set light to the wood fire with a taper brought from the nursery. " Now Charlotte," her aunt said, when that was done, "suppose you were to play over that piece of music which you said this morning you had forgotten. A quarter of an hour's practice would make it all right again !"

Charlotte looked rather unwilling, but she opened the pianoforte, and got her music; and though she began very languidly, her interest increased as she played, and in half an hour she could play the neglected piece very nicely.

" Will you wind this skein of blue silk for me ?" her aunt asked, almost before Charlotte had closed the pianoforte; "papa has got such a large hole in his purse, that if I do not make haste to net him a new one, he will lose all his money."

The skein was wound, and then Charlotte read aloud to her aunt some part of an historical review which was very interesting, and not too difficult for her to understand. She could hardly believe it possible when the clock on the chimney-piece struck half-past five, and the other children came running in to say that tea was ready.

"Oh, how quickly this afternoon has gone, and how pleasantly!" she added; "I do wonder why I feel so happy and merry now, for I was so dull and uncomfortable before!"

"You need not wonder long, dear," her aunt said; "you were dull and uncomfortable

because you were idle, doing good to nobody, and harm to yourself; and now you
are cheerful and happy, because you have
been active and busy. So now off to your
tea!"

They all ran to their tea, but very soon
came back; Charlotte carrying a cup of tea,
and Johnny a plate with a slice of bread and
butter.

" See, aunt Atta," Charlotte exclaimed,
" what we've brought you! Mossy said she
knew you had a headache, and so we thought
you would like some tea. And then if your
head isn't very bad, may we sit here with you
by the fire, and will you tell us a story?"

" You little monkeys, trying to bribe me
with tea!" aunt Atta said; "but you may stay.
with me, dears; though as to a story, I think

I told you all my poor head could furnish, during the measles time."

"Oh, but do recollect some more," Lizzie said; "tell us about yourself when you were a little girl, aunt Atta; that is what I like best of all!"

"But really, Lizzie," aunt Atta said, "I was not at all a wonderful little girl, and did not do many very remarkable deeds to tell of; and I suppose you do not want me to invent marvellous stories about myself."

"No, of course not," Lizzie answered; "but we don't want wonderful stories, we like to hear what you did and said, and all that sort of thing!"

"Well," aunt Atta said; "I will try. Let me see, — I think I can tell you, only it really is not a story, something that agrees with what Charlotte and I were saying about being discontented. Shall I tell you how I was once cured of being discontented?"

"You, aunt Atta? Were you ever discontented?" Charlotte asked in astonishment.

"Yes, indeed I was, Chatty, at a time when I had nothing to dissatisfy me, or make me otherwise than happy. Since that, I have had some real sorrows and trials, and I have learnt to be grateful to GOD for the many comforts and enjoyments He gives me, and even for the sorrows too."

Aunt Atta stopped speaking, as if her thoughts had wandered to past events; and Johnny was just going to ask her what sorrows and trials she had had, but Charlotte pulled his arm, and whispered.

" Hush, Johnny, don't ask aunt Atta questions about that.   Mossy says she knows she
has borne a great deal, and I don't think she
would like us to ask her."

" You have often heard me say how happily
we lived at home with your dear grandpapa,
papa and our brother Edmund and I; everything we wished for, we had, and no persons
could be happier.   But every now and then
I was apt to have fits of discontent, and wish
to change my circumstances, though I hardly
knew to what I would change.   These fits of
dissatisfaction generally came on when I was
less amused or pleased than usual.   The time
I am telling you about, was when I was
just seventeen, and my dear brother Edmund,
who you know is dead since then, and some
other friends I loved very much, had all

gone away that day, and I was very much depressed and out of spirits. There were several things I ought to have done; my dear father, too, missed his son, and I should have tried to amuse him, and prevent him from feeling lonely; I ought to have gone to the village school; and there were several cottages in the parish to which I had errands. But no, I indulged my depression, and sat over the fire; sometimes reading, but generally staring at the burning wood, and thinking how much I was to be pitied. All seemed so dull and unattractive; and I excused myself from doing my regular duties, because I had no inclination for them. At last, however, something whispered to me that this was wrong, and partly from that feeling, partly because I was tired of sitting over the fire,

I put on my bonnet and cloak, and went out in spite of a soft drizzling rain.

"The first cottage I went to, was an old woman's. She was tolerably well off, and had nobody to care for but herself, but still she was generally complaining. This day, when I gave her a bottle of medicine for her cough, the old story began—'Bless you, Miss Arden, I'm sure I need it! I'm always cough, cough, cough! I can rest neither day nor night, and I've not a bit of appetite; indeed, where is the good of appetite to poor folks as has nothing dainty to satisfy it with! And I'm so lonely, never a one to cheer me, and the neighbours do come and bother me so!' and so the querulous old body went on, making me feel quite angry at her discontent. I tried to reason with her, and point

out how much better off she was than many;
but she stopped me with, 'Ah! sure it's
well enough for you to talk, that's got
nothing to discontent you!' This set me
thinking, and I walked on, wondering whether
it was not worse in me to be discontented
than in old Jenny? My conscience said yes;
for I had really no cause for discontent.
But the lesson was completed in the next
visit, which was to a widow woman, with
several little children, who had hard work to
struggle on and support them all. I found
her very poorly herself, and two of the
children laid up, one with a scalded foot and
the other with a bad feverish cold. 'Eh,
poor dears,' the mother said, 'they must
have patience and be content. Indeed little
Peggy might have scalded both her feet,

which would have been a deal worse, and as to Jem, why he had a worse attack than this last year, and one of the neighbours has given him such nice black-currant tea, I tell him it's almost a good thing to be ill, and get such.'

" ' But you seem ill yourself.'

" ' Aye, ma'am, I've one of my bad headaches to day; they often come, but I lie down a bit when I can, and they get better with patience. They might be a deal worse.'

" ' Has Tom got the place as garden boy you were seeking ?'

" ' No, ma'am—he was too little; but I tell him, never mind, wait a bit patiently, and something good will turn up for him. GOD has always taken care of us, and He won't begin to leave off now, I think.'

" In this way the poor widow saw a gleam of brightness in everything, and I do believe that she was happier that day than I ; with all my advantages and blessings, she had one I wanted—a thankful heart. But that night, before I went to bed, I asked GOD to forgive me for my unthankfulness (after all, discontent is the same thing), and to help me never more to give way to it. Afterwards, when real troubles began to come on me, I often thought of the poor widow, and tried to trace GOD's Mercies through them, and that wonderfully lightens all troubles."

" I should so like—" Johnny began, but he stopped short.

" I think I can guess what you are going to say," aunt Atta said, kindly. " That you should like to know what my troubles were ;

but I cannot tell you that story now. By and by, when you grow older, perhaps I may; at present, you must be satisfied with knowing that one of my greatest happinesses is in living with my darling children and their dear papa and mama. And now I must run away, for Tiny will expect me to have her in my room before I dress for dinner."

The children stayed talking, and they agreed that aunt Atta could hardly have had any very great troubles, or she would not be so merry and cheerful as she now was. They did not know how those who receive everything as coming with Mercy from the Hand of an All-Wise and All-Loving Father, rise above their earthly sorrows, feeling themselves the more set apart and conse-

crated to GOD, and the more devoted to
their fellow-creatures. This it was, that
made aunt Atta so cheerful and lively with
the children; and she did not only *seem* so,
she really was happy, for she felt that the
" first-fruits " of her life had been dedicated
to GOD, and that, come what would, He
was always guarding and keeping her, so
nothing troubled her greatly; but she gather-
ed honey out of everything, even where it
seemed least likely. But the children agreed,
anyhow, that aunt Atta was very very dear,
and that they loved her with all their hearts.

CHAPTER IX.

The Visit.

THE visit to Mrs. Charlton, which had been looked to with so much pleasure, was only postponed, and one very fine morning they all set off for East Moor Vicarage, where she lived. Mr. Arden and Edmund rode, for his papa had hired a nice little pony for him from Winchester, and mama, aunt Atta, with Charlotte, Johnny, and Lizzie, went in the carriage.

Mr. and Mrs. Charlton had no children of their own, but they were both exceedingly

fond of children, and knew how to talk
and play with them, and make them happy.
They had been over to Eston Manor, and all
the little Ardens had been very much taken
with Mr. Charlton's merry good-nature, and
his wife's gentle winning smile, so that they
scarcely felt in the least shy now, in going to
see them.

They drove through a handsome park,
with very fine trees, and saw a herd of pretty
deer, who hardly seemed afraid of the carriage, and did not run far away. Then they
came to a gate, which was almost buried in
trees and shrubs, and just within, was
Mr. Charlton's house; such a pretty, irregu-
lar building, with large old chimney stacks,
and oriel windows, and curious carvings in
all corners. It was very much covered, too,

with creepers; some sweet roses, and other flowering plants, blossoming quite up to the bed-room windows.

The Ardens were warmly welcomed by their kind friends, and after a little while Mrs. Charlton proposed that the children should go and play about in the garden.

"I think they will be happiest alone," she said, "and I am quite sure they will not do any mischief. Perhaps, by and by, Mr. Arden and Mr. Charlton will take them for a walk into the Park—we have Even-song at four o'clock, and after that the great heat will be over."

"Oh, have you Even-song!" Johnny said, "how pleased mama and aunt Atta will be!"

Mrs. Charlton smiled, and from the side

window, she pointed to the church tower, which was quite close to the garden, and was a very fine old building.

Charlotte asked whether they might go into the church-yard, and Mrs. Charlton said that they might, as she was sure they would not run, or jump, or play there, as if it were not consecrated ground.

Then they all ran away, and very much they enjoyed going all over the pretty garden, and seeing Mrs. Charlton's large cage of canaries, where thirty or forty pretty little birds were hopping about. When they were tired of this, they went into the churchyard, and walked round it very quietly, and then sat down on a stone seat in the porch, which was shaded by a fine old yew tree.   There they began to talk of what they meant or wished to be hereafter.

Edmund said he meant to be a Priest, as good an one as Mr. Brantyre, and he should always look grave and serious as Mr. Brantyre did; but Lizzie declared that her dear Godpapa could laugh, and often did too very heartily; so Edmund said, "of course he didn't mean that he should never laugh, only he should look solemn in general, as a Priest ought to do."

He thought, though, that he would not have a London parish, but a beautiful country place, just like Mr. Charlton's at East Moor, and a handsome church, and everything so very nice. Nobody should be wicked in his parish!

Lizzie said she meant to marry, and have

a very great many little boys and girls, all as pretty and rosy as Walter, and she should do such wonderful things with them, as never were heard of before.

Johnny was to be a soldier; and when they asked Charlotte what she meant to be, she said that she thought probably it was best to wait and see what GOD appointed, but she fancied she should always like best to live at home with papa and mama, and to take great care of them when they grew old, and be a good maiden aunt to Lizzie's innumerable children, as aunt Atta was to them.

They went on talking over these plans till the church bells began to ring, and soon they saw Mr. Charlton come from the vicarage and go into the vestry by a side door, and a few minutes after their papa and mama, Mrs. Charlton and aunt Atta, all came, and the children went into church with them. Mrs Charlton was pleased to see how well they all behaved, and Johnny tried hard not to be distracted by the beautiful painted glass windows, at which he could not help wishing to look. When service was over, Mrs. Charlton took the children round, and let them look as much as they liked at the bright figures and colors; and Edmund and Charlotte, and even the younger ones, could tell what most of them meant, and knew a great many of the Saints too, with their different emblems.

When they left the church, all the party, except Mrs. Charlton and Mrs. Arden, went to walk in the park woods, where they collected all sorts of treasures; oak apples, blackberries, wood strawberries, and wild flowers, and, what they prized particularly, some wood-pigeon's feathers, and some of the pretty little pencilled blue feathers from the jay's wings. These were to be taken home for Tiny, as she was too little to come with them.

The children thought their walk quite too short, when Mr. Charlton said it was time to go back to the vicarage. There they found their mama and Mrs. Charlton sitting on the lawn.

Whilst the grown-up people dined, the children had tea in the drawing-room, and Charlotte poured it out. They thought the tea, and the home-made brown bread and butter, and the cherries, the very best they had ever tasted.

After tea they were all very much pleased with looking over a large book of drawings, and they found sketches of East Moor Church, and of the pretty vicarage, and several other places they knew.

All were quite sorry when nine o'clock struck, and the carriage was announced, but they liked sitting up so late, and the drive home by moonlight was a great pleasure. It was half-past ten when they got home, which delighted Johnny and Lizzie especially, as they had never been up so late before.

There were many other pleasures at Eston Manor. Edmund enjoyed his rides exceedingly; most particularly when he could come home and tell how he had leapt some small ditch, or how Laurel (so the little pony, which was bay-coloured, was called)

had kicked and jumped about without throwing him.   There was another pony, still
smaller, on which the other children rode
sometimes, and Lizzie and Johnny liked it
very much.   Charlotte was rather more
frightened.

They liked wandering about the heath,
and looking for what they called cornelians,
that is, any bright or transparent stones; and
papa laughed very much at the large geo-
logical collection which accumulated by
degrees.

Sometimes they went with their mama
and aunt to some of the neighbouring
cottages, and to the school, in a village not
far distant.   And one day, on Tiny's birthday, papa and mama dined early on purpose,
and they all had tea together in the large

veranda which went round the drawing-room windows. Aunt Atta made Tiny a wreath of pretty pink noisette roses, and she sat by her mama like a little queen.

Charlotte grew quite strong again in the fresh country air, and with a little determination and effort, took again to her occupations, and did not find she was at all less happy for doing some lessons every day, and all the games and walks were much pleasanter after she had been busy, and felt that she had earned some amusement.

CHAPTER X.

A Time of Trouble.

At last November came, and Mr. Arden was obliged to leave Eston Manor, where the children had been very happy, to go back to town. At first they were sorry, and began to grieve over the garden, and their walks and drives, and all their country pleasures. But Charlotte (who had tried hard to conquer her listless discontent, and often spoke of ' aunt Atta's widow'), began to remind them of the pleasures to which they were returning; their books and toys which were left in London; their cosy evening readings; the tea parties with aunt Atta when papa and mama dined out; going to church again in the week; and, best of all, seeing Mr. Brantyre again. Then they all agreed that though the country was very nice, and they had been very happy, still they should quite enjoy going home again.

It is a sad thing for those people (and I am afraid there are many), who grow up without learning to attach an almost magical delight to the word home. It will sometimes thrill through to the very heart, even of those who have long been separated from home and all that made it dear, and call them back from sin and shame.

It did not take long for all the party to get quite settled, and fall into their usual ways,

which were but little altered. Edmund was
not to go to school till after the next Easter
holidays; and though sometimes he fancied
that he wished to be a school-boy, still on the
whole, he was really glad to stay at home with
his brother and sisters.

The baby Walter had grown into a great
pet with every one; he was a remarkably
bright intelligent child; and being so much
talked to and played with by his brothers and
sisters, he took more notice than common for
his age, and would laugh and crow with
delight when any of them came to him. One
day when Charlotte went as usual to fetch
baby into her mama's room (she was so
steady and careful that she was allowed to
carry him, only not up or down stairs),
Moss said, as she put him into his sister's

arms, "I hope, poor darling, he'll be better amused in his mama's room than he is here, for he's been very fretful and uneasy. I don't think he can be well."

"Walter fretful, Mossy!" Charlotte said, almost vexed at any imputation on his disposition; "I never saw him cross yet!" and rather indignantly, she carried him away.

However, even Charlotte was obliged to own that baby was fretful that day. Nothing seemed to please him; he looked very pale, and often began to cry; though even then his mama or sisters could generally change the cry into a sweet smile.

Mrs. Arden thought he was cutting some teeth, and sent for Dr. Head, who was of the same opinion. That night baby seemed better. The next day, however, Charlotte was sitting reading to her mama, who was nursing baby, when suddenly she saw her mama turn very pale; and looking at baby, she saw that he was quite altered in his face. Charlotte was a sensible thoughtful little girl; she did not cry or scream, but she said directly, "Oh mama, what shall I do? shall I run and call Mossy?"

Mrs. Arden begged she would quickly, and in an instant Charlotte ran down to the servants' hall, where Moss and Emma were at dinner, and fetched them both, and then she went to aunt Atta, who also ran to the nursery.

A servant was sent directly for Dr. Head, and meanwhile baby was put into a hot bath, and everything tried that was likely to do him good. Charlotte crept into the nursery, and when she saw baby looking quite pale and altered, taking no notice of anybody, and her mama holding him, the tears in her eyes, though she was very quiet; and aunt Atta, Moss, and Emma, all looking very sad, she felt sure that baby was very ill indeed, and the tears came rushing into her eyes. However, she thought that it would distress her mama to see her cry, so she went away again, into the room where she and Lizzie and Tiny slept, and she knelt down beside her bed, and prayed to GOD not to let baby be so very ill, and make her mama so unhappy. Then when the tears seemed to have stopped, Charlotte went back to the nursery. Aunt Atta was standing near the window, so Charlotte went up to her and whispered—" Can I be of any use, aunt?"

" Yes, dear," her aunt said, " if you will go downstairs to the others, they are playing in the drawing-room, and if you will go and see after them, and try to keep them amused down there, you will be very useful, for they must not come upstairs at present. We must keep the nursery quiet."

Charlotte was just going to say that she would much rather be useful upstairs, where she could see and hear how baby went on, but she thought the right thing was to do at once what she was told, for Charlotte was now fast learning to act, not by inclination, but by duty.

So she went downstairs directly, and tried to do just what she thought her mama would like best; she told the others that baby was very ill, and that they were all to be quiet, and stay down in the drawing-room, and then she did not assume an air of authority over the others, and order them about, but she played nicely and kindly with Tiny, and kept her happy, though several times she began to want to go up to Mossy.

All the children were very sorry that baby was so ill, and they watched Dr. Head's carriage come and go with great eagerness. Edmund wanted to run to the nursery, to ask what he had said, but Charlotte said that she was sure mama would be better pleased for them to stay where they were, and she thought aunt Atta would come and tell them about baby soon, and she spoke so gently, that Edmund, who sometimes rebelled a little against being dictated to by Charlotte, was quite ready to do as she wished.

It was not long before aunt Atta came down, and she thanked the children for being so good and not troublesome. She said that baby was still very poorly indeed, but that he was better, and Dr. Head hoped to find him much better still, when he came at night. Aunt Atta said, too, that as they wanted to keep baby very quiet, the children were to have their tea downstairs, and not go up to the nursery without leave. So at the usual time the tea-things were brought into the drawing-room, and aunt Atta made tea for them there. Generally this would have been a great pleasure, but now they could not feel glad, because they were thinking of poor little Walter, and of their mama who was so anxious and unhappy.

Mrs. Arden did not come down to dinner,

and both their papa and aunt seemed out of spirits—the children felt sad too, and were very quiet. When they went up to bed their mama came out of the day-nursery to wish them good night, and said that she thought baby was really better.

Charlotte was the last to go to bed, and she asked her mama if she might not give baby one kiss. At first Mrs. Arden said, "No, he was asleep, and the least thing might disturb him," and so Charlotte was going without saying anything more, but just then, a little cry shewed that he was awake, and Mrs. Arden hurried back, telling Charlotte that she might follow.

She was very much grieved to see how ill dear little Walter looked; he had no color at all, and there were dark circles under his eyes, which generally were so sparkling and merry. He appeared quite awake now, and very restless; Charlotte took hold of one of his little hands, and spoke to him, "Walter! darling! Chatty's own Walter!"

Then baby opened his large blue eyes, and when he saw Charlotte, he quite knew her, and put out his arms to her, and smiled, but it was not like his usual merry laugh, and the change almost made his sister cry.

Her mama said she had better go to bed now; and so Charlotte went; but she was thinking too much of baby, and of her mama's pale anxious face, to go to sleep. Lizzie and Tiny were fast asleep, but after Emma had taken the candle away, Charlotte lay awake, thinking of Walter, and how quickly he had become ill, and the more she thought, the more certain she grew, that he was very ill, and that her parents and aunt and nurse thought so too. Charlotte felt as if she should never go to sleep; she listened and heard baby's voice once or twice, but the house was very still. Ten o'clock struck, and just then a carriage stopped at the door; and soon Charlotte heard a man's footstep on the stairs. She supposed it was Dr. Head; soon she heard her papa and aunt speaking very softly as they came up. Then again all was still. By and bye Charlotte heard Dr. Head go away, and she fancied her papa went down stairs with him. By this time she had grown so anxious and uneasy, that she felt as if she could not stay where she was any longer. Charlotte did not like, however, to go into the nursery, and startle her mama; but, jumping out of bed, she crept very quietly into her aunt's room, and determined to watch for her leaving the nursery.

It was cold weather, but there was a fire in aunt Atta's room, and Charlotte took a warm knitted shawl of her aunt's, and wrapped herself in it, and sat down on the rug before the fire to keep her feet warm, for she had no shoes or stockings on.

It seemed a long time, however, that no one came into the room, and Charlotte got more and more unhappy. " Perhaps baby is dying," she said to herself; " and I shall never see his dear merry face looking up and laughing at me again, or have his nice fat arms cuddling round my neck. Oh baby! dear dear baby! what can I do?" Then Charlotte remembered how baby had been made GOD's own little child at his baptism, and she re-collected all that was said about JESUS CHRIST taking the little children into His Arms, and blessing them; and she thought that Those Arms were around dear little Walter now; and then she tried to say over the hymn for Holy Innocents' Day in the *Christian Year*, which she had learned with aunt Atta; and she tried to recall all that her aunt had said to explain it, and now Charlotte quite under-stood and applied the verses,—

> " And next to these Thy gracious word
> Was as a pledge of benediction, stor'd
> For Christian mothers, while they moan
> Their treasur'd hopes, just born, baptised and gone.
> Oh, joy for Rachel's broken heart!
> She and her babes shall meet, no more to part;
> So dear to Christ, her pious haste
> To trust them in His Arms, for ever safe embraced.

" She does not grudge to leave them there,
   Where to behold them was her heart's first prayer,
   She does not grieve—but she must weep,
   As her pale placid martyr sinks to sleep,
   Teaching so well and silently
   How, at the Shepherd's call, the lamb should die ;
   How happier far than life the end
Of souls that infant-like beneath their burden bend."

Then Charlotte knelt down, and said the Lord's Prayer half aloud, and very slowly, and she thought she had never before quite understood what was meant by " Thy Will be done," but now she knew that in saying that, she meant, that darling baby should live or die as GOD saw best.

So she said it over again, and then she hid her face in the arm-chair, for the thought of baby's dying seemed almost more than she could bear.

Soon afterwards aunt Atta came into the room with a candle in her hand—she too looked pale and tired, and Charlotte saw that there were tears in her eyes.

At first her aunt did not see the little girl, nestled down upon the rug, and when she did, she appeared surprised. Charlotte looked up and said, " Oh, aunt Atta, I hope you are not angry with me for coming here, but I was so unhappy, I could not sleep, and I wanted so much to hear about baby. Is he—" and then poor Charlotte could not say any more, but burst into tears.

Aunt Atta had put down the candle, and now she sat down in the arm-chair, and lifted Charlotte on to her knee, and drew her very close to her breast, and did not try to stop her crying, for she thought the little

girl would be relieved by it, and she felt
sorry to think that she had been there, awake,
alone and unhappy.   Then she said in a low
voice, " Dear baby is very very ill, Chatty,
and Dr. Head thinks it right to tell us
that he fears he' may never get better, but
he still hopes he will.   Now, dearest Chatty,
I am telling you the real truth, because
I think you are a right-feeling little girl, and
will try to believe, that whatever GOD sees
best for dear little Walter, will be done, and
that even if He should take him away from us,
that it will be right."

Poor Charlotte could not help sobbing,
and some tears rolled down her aunt's face,
but she kissed Charlotte, and said, " It will
be very hard to bear, if it does please GOD
that our bright baby should die; and He is

not displeased with us for being very sorry, only we must try and be willing to give him up, if GOD sees fit to take him back."

"It would be so sad, never to hear him coo and crow again, or see him put out his little arms!" Charlotte said, and again her tears prevented her from speaking.

"Yes, it would," aunt Atta said, " and we should miss him sadly, especially poor mama, Chatty; but she is quite prepared to give him up, though she certainly does hope very much that he may not be taken from her. And for dear little Walter himself, we could not but be glad; glad that he should go to be with the bright happy Angels, who, in their shining garments, always are round the Throne of JESUS CHRIST, and sing His Praise. Now Walter is 'signed, sealed,

and blest,' and we know that he has done no
sin, and that since his Baptism he is God's
own child, and will be taken immediately to
happiness; but if he lives he may learn to do
wrong, and cannot be so holy and pure in
God's Sight.   And now, Chatty dear, I
want to go back to the nursery, because I
can be of some comfort and help to mama.
Shall you be happier now, and able to go to
sleep?"

"I don't think I can sleep, aunt Atta,
now," Charlotte said; "I cannot help thinking
so much about baby, and I shall want so to
hear about him.   Shall you sit up all night
with mama?"

"I do not know, dear, but would you like
it if I let you stay here in my bed, and then,
when I come back, I can tell you how baby is."

" Oh, yes !" Charlotte said, " that would be very nice ; I should feel nearer to baby here ; please let me stay, aunt Atta !"

So her aunt helped Charlotte to get into her bed, and made her promise to try and go to sleep, and although Charlotte thought that it was very unlikely that she should, she said she would try. Then her aunt went back to the nursery, and Charlotte lay looking at the bright fire, and thinking of baby and mama, and of what aunt Atta had said, till gradually she fell asleep; and when next her aunt came in, the little girl was sleeping quietly and comfortably.

The next morning, when Charlotte awoke, she felt puzzled at first as to where she was, and what had happened ; but in a minute she remembered all, and called to her aunt,

for it was early, and not full daylight yet.
No one answered, and Charlotte was just
going to get up and look for Emma to dress
her, when aunt Atta came into the room.
Charlotte felt quite afraid to ask about
Walter, lest she should hear that he was
dead ; but she exclaimed, "Oh ! aunt, tell
me !"

Aunt Atta came to the bedside directly,
and put her arms round Charlotte, as she
said with a smile, "I have good news, dear,
for you. It has pleased GOD to make our
little darling much better, he is sleeping very
sweetly now, and we have every reason to
believe that the danger is past. We must
thank GOD very gratefully indeed, for His
Goodness."

Charlotte felt so happy, so very happy,

that she began to cry, though she looked up at her aunt, and smiled to see that there were tears in her eyes too. " And poor mama?" Charlotte asked.

" You can fancy how relieved she is, and, as she has had such a very trying night, papa and I have persuaded her to go and lie down now a little, as baby really does not want her. And now, my Chatty, go and get dressed, for this is the last morning that we should like to miss Church, when we have so much to thank GoD for."

Charlotte went quickly to get ready, and Johnny came running up to say that papa had said, he and Lizzie should go to Church too, that morning. So they all went together, and all the children were very attentive, and when the Thanksgiving was said,

"Almighty GOD, Father of all Mercies, we
Thine unworthy servants do give Thee most
humble and hearty thanks for all Thy Goodness and Loving-kindness to us, and to all
men," Charlotte unfolded her hands, and slid
one into aunt Atta's hand.   Aunt Atta knew
that she meant that they had especial thanks
to return on that morning for dear baby's
preservation to them.

Mrs. Arden did not come down to
breakfast; but the children went to her
room, and as they were all very quiet,
they had a sight of little Walter, who was
sleeping comfortably, and looked more like
himself again, though he was still pale
and delicate.

They all seemed to prize the little fellow
more than ever from that time, and when-

ever the brothers and sisters were inclined to humour him too much, and let him have everything his own way, Mrs. Arden used to say, "No, no, we must not spoil Walter, for if we let him grow up into a self-willed boy, we shall perhaps some day have cause even to feel that it would have been better for him to have died when he was a little sinless baby, and sure to go to Heaven."

"We all love him far too much to spoil him, do we not, Aunt Atta?"

"Aunt Atta was a regular spoilt child herself," Mr. Arden said, laughing; "so she is the very last person who ought to say much about spoiling her nephews and nieces."

"Well, I hope we shall all be spoilt into something as nice as she is!" Lizzie said, giving her aunt a great hug; and one and all agreed, that if aunt Atta was spoilt, then spoiling was a very good thing; with which sapient decision, the " conclave" (as Edmund, who was growing very learned, called the little assembly) separated.

THE END.

RICHARDS, PRINTER, 100, ST. MARTIN'S LANE.

Tales of Kirkbeck; or, the Parish in the Fells.
By the Author of "Lives of Certain Fathers," &c. Second Edition, in
1 vol., cloth, 3s. 6d., or by post, 4s.
"We trust these tales will obtain the circulation they deserve, and be
but the forerunner of others from the same pen."—*Guardian.*

Lives of Certain Fathers of the Church in the
Fourth Century. Edited by the Rev. W. J. E. Bennett, M.A., late Student
of Christ Church, Oxford, and Perpetual Curate of S. Paul's, Knightsbridge. In 1 vol., fcap. 8vo., 6s., by post 6s. 6d.

The Second Volume of Lives of Certain Fathers
of the Church in the Fourth Century. Edited by the Rev. W. J E.
Bennett, M.A., late Student of Christ Church, Oxford, and Perpetual
Curate of S. Paul's, Knightsbridge. In foolscap 8vo.

The Navvies. By the same Author.
No. 1. HARRY JOHNSON. Price 3d.
No. 2. FRANK MEADE. Price 4d.

Aunt Atta, a Tale. By the Author of "Tales of
Kirkbeck; or, the Parish in the Fells." In one volume, royal 16mo.,
handsomely bound in cloth.

Holy Communion.—A Word about Servants on
the Subject of the Holy Communion, addressed to Masters and Mistresses.
Price one halfpenny, or 5d. per dozen.

Letters to my Children. Second Edition, with a
New Preface. 2 vols., post 8vo., price 15s.; or separately,—Vol. 1. CHURCH
SUBJECTS, 7s. 6d.; Vol. 2. MORAL SUBJECTS, 7s. 6d. By the Rev.
W. J. E. Bennett.
"The author of these letters is one of the most respected clergymen in
London, and his church at Knightsbridge is, without exception, the best
regulated in the metropolis. This being well known, it is not unnatural
that Mr. Bennett's book should be read with more than ordinary interest;
and it has fulfilled every expectation raised by its announcement. The
first volume comprises a series of letters on Church Subjects, and the
second a similar collection on Moral Subjects, both of which are written
in a pious, sensible, and zealous strain. The former portion is chiefly an
elucidation of the chief points connected with our Church: such, for
instance, as baptism, holy men, places, and times; and the latter contains
elaborate addresses on obedience to parents, and duty to inferiors; on
study, lying, the temper, pleasure, and choice of a profession. It is almost
impossible to enlarge on the many topics the author has introduced.
Some of the letters might be read advantageously by children of a larger
growth, for they have in them excellent and talented essays on the duties
of one man towards another. These books should be placed in the hands
of every young person, for golden lessons are scattered through their
pages."—*Durham Chronicle.*
"Mr. Bennett would have made short work of the Gorham Case if he
had had the controul of the Judicial Committee of the Privy Council.
He lays down the law pretty considerably in this volume."—*Atlas,*
Jan. 19th, 1850.

CPSIA information can be obtained
at www.ICGtesting.com
Printed in the USA
BVHW041548030719
552601BV00012B/247/P